THE WAY OF PRAYER

FATHER GABRIEL OF
ST. MARY MAGDALEN, O.C.D.

The Way of Prayer

A Commentary on
Saint Teresa's *Way of Perfection*

~

Translated by
THE CARMEL OF BALTIMORE

SECOND EDITION

IGNATIUS PRESS   SAN FRANCISCO

This book was originally published in Italy under the title *La Via dell'Orazione* by the Carmel of St. Joseph in Rome, 1955.

The original English edition was published by Spiritual Life Press, Milwaukee, Wisconsin, 1965.

Nihil obstat:

Rev. John E. Twomey, S.T.L., Ph.D.
Censor Librorum

Imprimatur:

+ William E. Cousins, D.D.
Archbishop of Milwaukee
August 24, 1965

Cover art:
Saint Teresa of Avila
Alonso del Arco (1635–1704)
Museo Lazaro Galdiano
© Mondadori Portfolio/Electa/Art Resource, New York

Cover design by Roxanne Mei Lum

Published in 2017 by Ignatius Press, San Francisco
All rights reserved
ISBN 978-1-58617-129-2
Library of Congress Control Number 2016941444
Printed in the United States of America ∞

The Discalced Carmelite Nuns of Baltimore offer this translation as an expression of their gratitude to God, to the Virgin of Carmel, and to their holy mother, Saint Teresa of Jesus, on the occasion of the one hundred seventy-fifth anniversary of the founding of their Carmel.

Contents

PART IV

THE LIFE OF PERFECTION

*Based on Saint Teresa's
Commentary on the Our Father*

Acknowledgments

Quotations from Saint Teresa are taken from vols. 1 and 2 of *The Collected Works of St. Teresa of Avila*, translated by Kieran Kavanaugh, O.C.D., and Otilio Rodriguez, O.C.D., and published by ICS Publications, Institute of Carmelite Studies, Washington, D.C., in 1976 and 1980.

Quotations from Saint John are taken from *The Collected Works of St. John of the Cross*, translated by Kieran Kavanaugh, O.C.D. and Otilio Rodriguez, O.C.D., and published by ICS Publications, Institute of Carmelite Studies, Washington, D.C., in 1979.

All quotations are reprinted here with the permission of the publisher.

PART I

SAINT TERESA'S IDEA

I

The "Way of Perfection"

In none of her other works did Saint Teresa portray more clearly and sublimely the contemplative ideal of intimacy with God as it employs prayer and penance for an apostolic purpose.

Saint Teresa was given the mission to teach the way to contemplative prayer and to restore to Carmel its ideal of prayer. So, with that practicality mystics have, she interested a few individuals and began a reform. Her nuns, seeing her so favored in prayer, asked her to teach them to pray . . .

Now, although the Saint inaugurated a reform in her Order, she also gave a new idea to all Christians. She taught that contemplative prayer should be aimed entirely at the apostolate. Her innovation was to unite not only prayer and the apostolate, but contemplation and the apostolate; for contemplation is a particular kind of prayer, which tends toward the most sublime intimacy with Our Lord.

No one can doubt that a contemplative person, as a friend of God, has power over His Heart; Saint Teresa aimed at raising an army of contemplatives to aid the Church.

Seeing Saint Teresa at prayer was enough to make one desire contemplation; that was why her first companions asked her to teach them the way to it. The apostles made the same request of Jesus: "Teach us to pray" (Lk 11:1). Jesus answered by teaching the *Pater noster*; Saint Teresa responded through this book, which contains her commentary upon that great prayer. It is not surprising that Saint Teresa answered as Jesus did, since the saints are dynamic members of the Mystical Body of Christ, sharing His life most intimately.

As Saint Luke reports, and also Saint Matthew, but more at length, in the Sermon on the Mount, Jesus first taught the dispositions for prayer, then what we should ask for.

The dispositions are: "When you pray, go into your room and shut the door and pray to your Father who is in secret; and your Father who sees in secret will reward you" (Mt 6:6). When Christ teaches prayer, He insists upon quiet retirement in order to pray well. Away from creatures one can speak in secret, and in secret the Father can answer. Saint Teresa said that God speaks to the heart when it is the heart that prays and that the more perfect prayer becomes, the more silent it is.

Then Jesus taught what we should ask: in this solitude, pray thus: "Our Father who art in heaven. . . ."

And what did Saint Teresa do but repeat this teaching? She wrote for those who seek contemplation. So, the first part of her book explains how the necessary disposition for it is to create in oneself the atmosphere of solitude through the practice of fraternal charity, detachment, and humility. "Had you asked about meditation I could have spoken about it and counseled all to practice it even though they do not possess the virtues, for meditation is the basis for acquiring all the virtues. . . . But contemplation is something else, daughters."[1] Like Jesus, she said detachment is necessary,

---

[1] Saint Teresa of Jesus, *The Way of Perfection*, in vol. 2 of *The Collected Works*

but she said it in a way especially directed to contemplatives. Then, like Jesus, she gave the prayer itself and taught how to recite the Our Father.

~

In the first chapters, Teresa sketched the contemplative ideal and showed that it is the traditional ideal of the Carmelite Order. Then she taught the practice of prayer, commenting on the Our Father and using it to portray a whole lifetime of prayer. Vocal prayer, she began, should be an intimate contact with God, an intimacy that trusts in the heavenly Father. In her pages on the first words of the *Pater*, she noted the childlike atmosphere Jesus created when He taught us to say "Our Father" to God. "Who art in heaven": here she taught the prayer of recollection, wherein one seeks a deep awareness of God's indwelling within him. The prayer of recollection is the most intimate prayer that we can reach by our own efforts; in it one puts himself at God's disposal. Then Our Lord, in the prayer of quiet, enters the soul and, in the prayer of union, draws the person to Himself. "Thy kingdom come, Thy will be done": the Saint recalled that these two things must go together if we want God to take possession of us through the prayer of quiet and of union. And if He takes possession of us, He also gives Himself to us. He enters the soul by the door of the will, so she added: "Let's give Him the jewel once and for all, no matter how many times we have tried to give it before" (*W* 162). And

---

of St. Teresa of Avila, trans. Kieran Kavanaugh, O.C.D., and Otilio Rodriguez, O.C.D. (Washington, D.C.: ICS Publications, Institute of Carmelite Studies, 1980), 94 (hereafter abbreviated as *W*).

she reminded us that giving to God is bound to be painful; but she knew how to make us esteem suffering: "See . . . what He gave to the one He loved most. . . . To those He loves more, He gives more of these gifts" (*W* 162). And the braver He sees a person, the more He gives him to suffer: "He gives according to the courage He sees in each and the love each has for His Majesty" (*W* 162). One who reaches the last dwelling places of the *Interior Castle* offers himself to God; God gives Himself more and more in return—these are the rich graces of the union of conformity. Then, when the soul's gift really becomes complete, God takes possession of it. This is the union Saint John of the Cross calls "transfiguring union". This is how Teresa sketched the path to union with God, begun by us with the gift of the will, and His gradual approach to us in order to take possession of us and draw us to Himself.

We need strength to make this gift a complete one, since it does involve suffering: "Give us this day our daily bread", bread to strengthen the soul. "Forgive us our trespasses": what need of pardon those living in intimacy with God always have! It is easy to fall into many little faults, but the contemplative is the one who tries hardest to avoid them, especially those of charity or forgiveness of small acts of discourtesy. "As we forgive those who trespass against us": a contemplative does not take offense if people fail to heed him. And then, since we carry our treasure in fragile vessels, we need protection: "Lead us not into temptation." The Saint taught that the safeguard against temptation is the love and fear of God.[2] Saint John of the Cross defined this fear as the perfect fear of the child, born of love for the

---

[2] Ibid., chapter 40, pp. 192–95.

Father.[3] In order not to displease his heavenly Father, a son
of God looks where he is going and seeks guidance to keep
from leaving the right road. "But deliver us from evil,"
from this earth, to go where good alone reigns. But even
here we must have an attitude of the greatest abandonment.
"The desires and impulses for death, which were so strong,
have left me . . . for I resolved to live very willingly in order to render much service to God", said the Saint, though
she longed for God, especially in those moments when she
glimpsed "through the lattices" a still greater love awaiting
her, "when no matter how much I try to reject the desire
to see Him, I cannot."[4]

Hence in Saint Teresa's writings we have a contemplative
commentary on the Our Father, showing how persons sincere in leading the interior life might become contemplatives or better still, intimate friends of God who draw down
graces upon the Church.

The Different Manuscripts

When she wrote the *Way of Perfection*, Saint Teresa was concerned only with her little convent in Avila and wrote only
for that small group, for she had no thought of any other
foundation. But then (1567) the General of the Order saw

[3] Saint John of the Cross, *The Spiritual Canticle*, stanza 26, no. 3, in *The
Collected Works of St. John of the Cross*, trans. Kieran Kavanaugh, O.C.D., and
Otilio Rodriguez, O.C.D. (Washington, D.C.: ICS Publications, Institute
of Carmelite Studies, 1979), 511.

[4] Saint Teresa of Jesus, *Spiritual Testimonies*, no. 17, in vol. 1 of *The Collected
Works of St. Teresa of Avila*, trans. Kieran Kavanaugh, O.C.D., and Otilio Ro-
driguez, O.C.D. (Washington, D.C.: ICS Publications, Institute of Carmelite
Studies, 1976), 329.

how useful it would be for Teresa's work to spread and ordered her to found other convents. She left that very year for
Medina del Campo and took her *Way of Perfection* with her.
But the Avila nuns must have insisted so strongly on having the first copy back that Teresa made another in her own
hand. So there are two autographs of the *Way of Perfection*:
one written at Saint Joseph's of Avila, which is preserved
at the Escorial with many other of the Saint's manuscripts,
and the other at the Carmelite convent in Valladolid.

The latter, which seems to have been written not later
than 1569, differs somewhat from the first. Comparing the
texts we see that the first is more familiar in style, the second more accurate; but it is also evident that the Saint had
the first manuscript before her when she wrote the second.
But, since she had composed it herself, she changed it freely;
intuitive as she was, she could not refrain from improving
it as her thought developed. The first was directed to her
daughters at Saint Joseph's in Avila; now she wrote with an
eye to the foundations of the future and, almost in spite of
herself, to all who long for the fountain of living water.

Saint Teresa also corrected and signed copies that were
made later, and a number of these still exist. Then, there
is an unsigned manuscript (at Toledo) that contains many
important corrections because it was slated for the printers.
A friend of hers, who esteemed her writings, Don Teutonio de Braganza, Archbishop of Evora, promised to edit
it, as we gather from a letter of the Saint's accompanying
the manuscript. She adds that it was one of the most intelligent of her nuns who helped prepare this manuscript. In
1580, Don Teutonio checked the printer's proofs, but Saint
Teresa did not have the consolation of seeing her work published, for it saw the light only in 1583, the year after her
death. Two years later, there was a second edition directed by

Father Gracian. The Valencian edition followed (1586), and in 1588 the complete edition of her *Works* by Luis de Leon appeared. Then it spread to other countries, translated first into French, later into Italian. Up to our own day there has been a continual succession of translations.

The autographs (Escorial, Valladolid, and Toledo) differ somewhat from each other. That of Valladolid is arranged best. Though it has forty-four chapters, there are only forty-two in modern editions; a note in the Toledo manuscript after chapter 4 reads: "there should not be a chapter here"; in addition, Teresa tore some pages out of the Valladolid manuscript—those on the game of chess, formerly chapter 17; this leaves forty-two chapters. Later we shall discuss Teresa's reasons for removing chapter 17. Later editors took it from the Escorial manuscript and reinserted it, since it does throw much light on the concept of the *Way of Perfection*.

If Carmel's Reformer wrote two copies of the *Way of Perfection* herself and then had other copies made and herself checked them, it is because she considered the book important. So aware was she of its value that, wishing to follow the Church's teaching in everything, she had it examined by eminent theologians, among them Spain's greatest at the time, Dominic Bañez. Her future biographer, Yepes, also examined it, and to him she confided one day that a theologian had told her that her writing "seemed to be Sacred Scripture" (that is, in it one felt divine inspiration!). It was the humble Teresa who spoke thus, the humble Teresa who knew she was nothing but knew also how mercy loves to stoop to little ones: "The mercies of the Lord I will sing forever!" was a favorite ejaculation of hers. In the humble little book she had written not for herself but for her daughters, God had helped her, and she realized that it had divine inspiration: not the kind recognized by the Church for

Sacred Scripture, yet real inspiration. God did not allow her to see the little work printed, but He did give her the joy of having it approved and praised by learned theologians.

Plan of the Book

In this work Saint Teresa included all the elements of Carmelite education and all the aspects of a life based on prayer. The first three chapters are complete in themselves and give a general view of the ideal of Teresa's reform. All the rest of the book indicates the road to perfection and invites the traveler to the fountain of living water (that is, contemplation).

From the fourth to the fifteenth chapters, Teresa wrote about the necessary moral foundation, which is the practice of heroic virtue leading to total detachment and complete gift of self. This is the only atmosphere in which contemplation can develop. Next comes a part—chapters 16 to 25 —that might be entitled "the prayer that leads to contemplation". Here the Saint insisted on two points: (1) we must resolve to search for the fountain of living water all our life, and (2) mental prayer should always be a spiritual contact with God.

With chapter 26 she came to particulars and began to comment on the petitions of the *Pater noster*, explaining the various degrees of prayer until the end of chapter 31. But when she wrote about the words: *Fiat voluntas tua*, though she continued to comment on the *Pater*, she went back to speaking of the perfect life that should accompany prayer so that it may be fruitful; she continued writing in this vein to the end of the book.

II

Carmel's Apostolate

In the first three chapters of the *Way of Perfection*, Saint Teresa set forth the apostolic side of Carmel's vocation. But she did not forget its traditional contemplative ideal: to offer God a love-filled heart prepared to receive from Him the gift of contemplation. She knew this ideal well and set it before her daughters early in the book, for it is the goal of the way of perfection she was describing. In doing so, however, she brought it out in its relationship to their apostolic duties. Never before had these obligations been expressed so vigorously.

Carmel, today a mendicant Order, was originally purely contemplative. The apostolate was always present, of course, but the way it developed when the Order came to the West and was numbered among the mendicants served to emphasize the Order's apostolic duties. Saint Teresa recognized this and responded by teaching the virtues characteristic of the mendicant life.

What are the mendicant Orders in the Church? They are the Orders that add the active life to the search for union with God. They are the Orders of mixed life, and in theological language they are also called apostolic Orders because such was precisely the life of the apostles, to whom they look for example in their work for souls. Franciscans, Dominicans, Augustinians, Servites, Carmelites are all members of apostolic Orders. They are called *mendicant* because they introduced into the Church (in the thirteenth century) a new form of religious life based on a more austere poverty, even in common, than had been practiced up to then. The ancient monks did renounce private ownership, but in common they had considerable possessions. The mendicant Orders renounced possessions even in common or reduced them to a minimum, to be freer for the service of souls to which the Church called them. They lived on alms from the faithful, but they repaid the faithful by preaching and administering the sacraments.

This definition of mendicant Orders casts light on the first three chapters of the *Way of Perfection*. The first and third speak directly of the apostolic vocation based on union of the soul with God; the third insists in particular on a proximate object of the apostolate: prayer and penance on behalf of priests, theologians, preachers, confessors, and so on. The second chapter is not a digression, as it might appear at first sight, for it goes back to one of the basic principles of Carmelite life: the poverty that is a necessary part of apostolic life.

Contemplation and Apostolate

The title of the first chapter, "The reason I founded this monastery with such strict observance" (*W* 41), does not indicate the whole content of the chapter but only the underlying thought, that is, an urgent desire to save souls. In other words, the apostolic ideal motivated Saint Teresa to give her Order its austere character.

~

Carmel, eremitical in its origin, had become an apostolic Order by the will of the pope when it came to Europe. After this change, it strove to balance the different elements making up its life, and various reforms within the Order show that such balancing was not easy.

Saint Teresa's reform—like several other reforms of the Carmelite Order—was a return to a more intense contemplative life; but her love for the ancient contemplative ideal did not make the Saint forget that her Order was an apostolic one. God had given her great love for souls and deep pity for those living in sin. The vision of hell she had before writing this work further sharpened these sentiments.[1] So it was to be expected that she would insist on the apostolate when teaching her daughters the fundamentals of their life.

"When I began to take the first steps toward founding this monastery . . . , it was not my intention that there be so much external austerity or that the house have no income; on the contrary, I would have desired the possibility that nothing be lacking. In sum, my intention was the intention of the weak and wretched person that I am—although I did have some good motives besides those involving my own comfort" (*W* 41). At first Saint Teresa did not think of anything but finding some quiet place where they could give themselves to contemplation more easily. But something happened . . .

---

[1] Let us note that when Saint Teresa says she wishes to return to the primitive rule in her reform, she does not mean the Rule of Saint Albert (1209), which was exclusively contemplative, but the rule of Pope Innocent (1247), which states that the organization of Carmel now becomes a mendicant, apostolic Order.

"At that time news reached me of the harm being done in France and of the havoc the Lutherans had caused and how much this miserable sect was growing. The news distressed me greatly, and, as though I could do something or were something, I cried to the Lord and begged Him that I might remedy so much evil. It seemed to me that I would have given a thousand lives to save one soul out of the many that were being lost there" (*W*41). This goaded her into making her religious family completely austere and poor. Numerous chapters of her *Way* treat of these characteristics.

We may ask ourselves what kind of apostolate Saint Teresa wished to live. The Carmelite apostolate is based on a fervent inner life that makes the soul powerful over the Heart of God. This power comes from the total gift of self, made as perfect as possible by means of the evangelical counsels. Carmelites are entirely devoted to Our Lord, sparing nothing in order to give to Him. These expressions of completeness, of totality—which we find also in the works of Saint John of the Cross—show how high Saint Teresa's ideal was.

The first thing needed to move the Heart of God and help save souls is to become intimate with Him. This friendship makes one's prayer and penance powerful, and prayer and penance are the interior tools of the apostolate.

> All my longing was and still is that since He has so many enemies and so few friends that these few friends be good ones. As a result I resolved to do the little that was in my power; that is, to follow the evangelical counsels as perfectly as I could and strive that these few persons who live here do the same. I did this trusting in the great goodness of God, who never fails to help anyone who is determined to give up everything for Him. My trust was that if these Sisters matched the ideal my desires had set for them, my

faults would not have much strength in the midst of so many virtues; and I could thereby please the Lord in some way. (*W* 41–42)

Pleasing Our Lord, one becomes dear to His Heart; then prayer will really have power. "Since we would all be occupied in prayer for those who are the defenders of the Church and for preachers and for learned men who protect her from attack, we could help as much as possible this Lord of mine who is so roughly treated by those for whom He has done so much good" (*W* 42). So the tools of the Carmelite apostolate—prayer and penance—get their power from the soul's love for God.

Saint Teresa had mentioned the immediate object of her apostolate in the words just quoted (that is, for whom she wished to pray); in the third chapter she did so again but at greater length. She wished to obtain the highest graces for all who defend the Church. But these defenders exist for the souls who make up the Church; hence, she said she wished to pray for the conversion of sinners, for the salvation of souls. "O my Sisters in Christ, help me beg these things of the Lord. This is why He has gathered you together here. This is your vocation. These must be the business matters you're engaged in. These must be the things you desire, the things you weep about; these must be the objects of your petitions" (*W* 42).

Teresa's first intention, the most important, was the salvation of souls. Other intentions were not excluded, but there is an immense difference between worldly matters and the apostolic intention proper to Carmel. "Your petitions [must] not, my Sisters, [be for] the business matters of the world" (*W* 42). and she went into particulars. She allowed praying for any good intention, and it may even be a duty toward benefactors to do so, but she made a sharp distinction between intentions of a temporal kind and this special intention. "For I laugh at and am even distressed about the things they come here to ask us to pray for: to ask His Majesty for wealth and money—and this is done by persons who I wish would ask Him for the grace to trample everything underfoot. They are well intentioned, and in the end we pray for their intentions because of their devotion —although for myself I don't think the Lord ever hears me when I pray for these things" (*W* 42–43).

"Indeed, were I not to consider the human weakness that is consoled by receiving help in time of need (and it is good that we help in so far as we can), I'd be happy only if people understood that these are not the things they should be begging God for with so much care" (*W* 43).

"The world is all in flames; they want to sentence Christ again, so to speak" (*W* 43).

Saint Teresa lived the truth of the Mystical Body of Christ; she understood Our Lord's words to Saint Paul on the road to Damascus: "Why do you persecute me?" (Acts 9:4). Like the apostle, she felt with the Church: to persecute the Church is to persecute Jesus; to do good to the Church is to do good to Jesus, to extend His Mystical Body and make it glorious.

> O my Redeemer, my heart cannot bear these thoughts without becoming terribly grieved. . . . Indeed, my Lord, one who withdraws from the world nowadays is not doing anything. Since the world so little appreciates You, what do we expect . . . , those of us who through the goodness of the Lord are freed of that contagious, scabby sore, that sect whose followers already belong to the devil? Indeed, they have won punishment with their own hands and have eas-

ily earned eternal fire. . . . Still, my heart breaks to see how many souls are lost. Though I can't grieve so much over the evil already done—that is irreparable—I would not want to see more of them lost each day. (*W* 42)

The apostolate was urgent in Saint Teresa's time, in the flood of Protestantism, but it is no less urgent now, in the flood of secularism and organized atheism. The Church's enemies are powerful and organized. But she has many fervent friends, too, and it is they who can acquire power over the Heart of God.

Poverty

The mendicant Orders live in poverty in order to be free to serve souls anywhere. And the very fact that they receive their livelihood from the people obliges them to the apostolate. Hence there is a close connection between poverty and the apostolate, and, consequently, the second chapter of the *Way* (which Saint Teresa devoted to the study of poverty) does not seem a digression injected between the two that present the apostolate.

She recalled the Gospel concept of poverty, showed how praiseworthy it is, and drew the consequences. The Gospel points the way to freeing oneself from everything: "Sell what you possess and give to the poor, and you will have treasure in heaven; and come, follow me."[2] But there is more than that to holy poverty. Material goods give an assurance for the future; one cannot throw away one's security in life without substituting something better. If a person were not convinced that God would take care of him, he

[2] Cf. Mt 19:21–Mk 10:21–Lk 18:22.

would act like a fool if he renounced all future security. So Our Lord began to speak of the birds and lilies (Mt 6:25–34) when He taught us poverty. "Look at the birds of the air: they neither sow nor reap nor gather into barns, and yet your heavenly Father feeds them. Are you not of more value than they?" "And why are you anxious about clothing? Consider the lilies of the field, how they grow." Saint Teresa believed and was sure that Our Lord would take care of her daughters if they were good nuns occupied with His interests; so she told them not to be anxious about people's gifts.

She insisted on liberty of spirit in matters of sustenance, and, first of all, on not being anxious about whether there will *be* any food or not. Little can be said after that! She asked a great deal: never to follow those little natural impulses that are so much a part of us.

∽

Saint Teresa had been carried away by enthusiasm in singing the praises of poverty; she admitted she had not realized it and added: "But since I have written this, . . . keep in mind that holy poverty is our insignia" (*W* 46). As long as she lived, she said, she would never cease repeating this, but it was well to have it written down so that her daughters would remember it after her death.

One advantage of poverty, she pointed out, is that it gives dominion over all the world. Among men distinction is measured by wealth. Certainly the recognition today given labor marks human progress: people ought to be respected more for their labor than for their possessions. But our society still suffers from this evil, and honor goes to money; and so arises the anxiety to get it in order to make one's way in the world. But what we need is to let go of earthly things; Saint Teresa had good reason to praise poverty.

Another advantage she saw in this virtue was that it was a safeguard for the spiritual life, a protection from everything that could impede flight toward God. So often religious Orders have lost their fervor by weakening the practice of poverty.

A final advantage, she said, was that the monastery's poverty was an opportunity to practice that apostolate of which she spoke in the first chapter. The nuns should help others by means of prayer, and they would receive aid without seeking it. God would move hearts to send them the necessities of life. They should be grateful to Him and repay their benefactors by their apostolate of prayer and meritorious work. It is a custom in Teresian monasteries to pray together for the benefactors each evening at the end of supper, after the alms have been read out. Saint Teresa exhorted the nuns earnestly to obtain their benefactors' spiritual welfare by their prayers. In so doing, they would also give God the glory flowing from these souls' well-being.

For the Priesthood

The third chapter of the *Way of Perfection* returns to Carmel's chief purpose: to help the Church's apostolate by prayer for graces needed. It begins by looking at the best strategy for the apostolate and at the priesthood's place in it. Teresa was thinking of her own tormented century when she wrote, but the best plan for spiritual conquest is still the same today, and everyone is convinced that to win the world back to Christianity we need to create a select group. This must be done especially among the official apostles, for though others collaborate in apostolic work, they are always inspired by its official promoters. Today, the laity's collaboration with the hierarchy's apostolate is insisted upon more than in Saint Teresa's time, for in those days no environment was closed to the priest. Today the sign "Entrance Forbidden" on factory doors and elsewhere keeps priests out of the places where youth are facing serious dangers. Into these places the official minister of Jesus Christ cannot penetrate, and here the layman's apostolate must develop. Hence, all that Saint Teresa desired to do for priests applies also to those who work in union with the hierarchy.

From the Middle Ages on, the common people have been going farther and farther from Christ; today huge masses are ignorant of the Faith. A reconquest is needed, and that will require intelligence and virtue. Our glance, with the Saint, turns mainly toward priests. She did well in specifying preachers and theologians. Not only those who distribute doctrine to the faithful, but also (and in the first place) those who by arduous study—not possible for preachers—fathom its depths, giving preachers by their books the bread of doctrine they must distribute.

And this is all the more necessary as we are exposed to error by human limitations; so much effort is required to get at the truth. There have always been heresies in Holy Church, and there are some now: tendencies from which we like to think ourselves freed are still alive. After Pius X's effective work against Modernism, we thought it dead, but it is raising its head again, and danger is felt here and there. The theologian has the high mission of trying to preserve the Church's heritage intact and of displaying it in all its vigor and beauty. He applies doctrine to the actual conditions of life for the guidance of all souls: from those just beginning to live the moral life to those reaching the heights of sanctity.

The Saint showed keen intuition in fixing attention first on theologians and then on preachers. If Christian doctrine were well preached, it would draw the crowds, but ignorance makes people dislike the Church. So many poor workmen allow themselves to be taken in by socialism and communism because they are unaware of the beauty of Christ's teachings. In 1936 in France, when the Communists offered to collaborate with the Catholics, there was some reciprocal contact, and in a meeting of two Communists with a Dominican Father, the priest gave the encyclicals *Rerum novarum* and *Quadragesimo anno* to the Communists. The two came back in a few days after reading them with the comment, "You are idiots to have such beautiful social doctrines and not see that they are lived out." These doctrines are too little known even by Catholics. They arouse real enthusiasm among workmen when presented to them in their own language, with examples from their own lives. But that means there must be men to study them and others to present them to the people. This is the work of theologians and preachers. And it is plain that the more educated laity can collaborate in making these teachings known.

We said there is always danger of error; to show it as error requires learned men. There is need to pray that these men may destroy it in time.

~

The priesthood's prominent role in winning people back to Christ justifies Saint Teresa's desire to establish this specially prepared group. She points out to the Carmelite nuns two things to seek in their prayers for priests: that they *be* holy and that they *remain* holy amid the dangers of the apostolate.

First of all, priests must be holy, for one holy man can do more than many who are not holy. Today there is a thirst for holiness among priests as well as an effective education for it. Through the priest's holiness, and his consequent generosity, Jesus Christ distributes the means of holiness to others. During His mortal life, Jesus taught, trained His disciples, and instituted the sacraments. The priest does the same: he teaches the Church's doctrine; he rules and trains his parish, his diocese, or the whole Church (the pope), and by spiritual direction he also trains souls. He administers the sacraments, from baptism to the Eucharist. All this is related to his holiness. The preaching of a holy priest will move hearts; an enlightened director will make souls recognize what God wills; a generous priest will know how to bear fatigue in administering the sacraments.

People are won when Christian doctrine is presented as attractively and clearly as it deserves. Thus, Saint Teresa says, we must pray that priests be holy.

And we must also ask God that they remain so, for in their ministry they must continually be in contact with the world. They need a matured spirit of mortification not to surrender to the satisfactions their life may offer, satisfactions of heart, of mind, and of honor; if they should, they would no longer be channels of supernatural life but would remain God's instruments only in a material sense. In particular, priests need to obey, for sure guidance comes from Rome, and when one no longer wishes to hear her venerable voice, there is danger of going astray.

Saint Teresa taught prayer by her own example, and she gave good example by praying as a member of the Mystical Body together with her sisters and with Jesus, the Head. It is splendid to see the doctrine of the Mystical Body lived thus at a time when it was not much spoken of. It was always a vital part of the Church's teaching, and Saint Teresa loved the Church so much that her devotion was aroused by whatever was essential in her doctrine.

And here a thought, expressed repeatedly in the course of this chapter, reappeared: we must become fit to obtain from God what we pray for. *Fit*, that is, pleasing to God and able to mediate with the Heart of God. And the only way a creature can please God is to do His will. Teresa had just proposed a life of complete self-denial; here was the root of the effectiveness of Carmel's prayer. She did not make positive statements; rather, she spoke as if simply manifesting a desire. But her intuition made her desire what Pope Pius XI confirmed in the Bull *Umbratilem* of 1924, where we read the following: "Much more is contributed to the growth and development of the Church by contemplative groups than by those who perform the actual labors, for it is they who call down from heaven the vivifying graces to irrigate the plowed fields of the other apostolic workers."[3] The Holy Father clearly states here that the external apostolate would be less fruitful if these souls did not exist. They do much more, he says unhesitatingly, than those who dedicate themselves to apostolic activity.

This asserts the need for purely contemplative Orders in the Church, even from a simply apostolic point of view, and confirms Saint Teresa's intuition. She spoke with her daughters in mind, but *the same is true of everyone who gives himself entirely*, so that God regards him with pleasure.

She ended the chapter with a general glance at Carmelite life, in which everything should have this apostolic aim:

[3] A.A.S. 16 (1924), 385.

"And when your prayers, desires, disciplines, and fasts are not directed toward obtaining these things I mentioned, reflect on how you are not accomplishing or fulfilling the purpose for which the Lord brought you here together" (*W* 52). At this high target Saint Teresa would have her followers aim; she wished them to have vast desires. And what desire is greater than the all-absorbing one for the salvation of souls, the very purpose Our Lord Jesus Christ had in the Redemption, to give and to increase in all men the life of the most holy Trinity?

PART II

THE ATMOSPHERE
OF CONTEMPLATION

I

Mutual Love

In this second part of the *Way of Perfection*—from chapter 4 to chapter 16—Saint Teresa described the virtues that detach the soul from creatures and render it interiorly free to receive the gift of contemplation and to be united to God.

To surround the soul with the atmosphere favorable to contemplation, she began by establishing a principle: if we wish to enter into intimate friendship with God in order to obtain graces for the Church, we must declare our love to Him and prove it by responding to its demands.

Then, if it is true that mortification draws its strength from prayer, the opposite is also true, namely, that prayer grows strong through mortification, for it finds in mortification the support it needs to become contemplation. The Saint, therefore, established the principle that prayer cannot be accompanied by self-indulgence. Of these two means employed by the contemplative life like two wings to rise to God, the more important is prayer; but, experience proves that mortification defends prayer, and in this respect I am of the opinion that mortification is the more important.

A person who does not cultivate mortification will not be a man of prayer; if a person, a community, or a congregation loses the spirit of mortification, it loses the foundation of

prayer. How necessary it is, then, to foster the habit of deny-
ing our whims for natural satisfaction and comfort. Without insistence on the practice of mortification, our natural
appetite for satisfaction awakens and makes its demands.

Mortification in material matters has to be emphasized
today when everywhere the spiritual is neglected. If we do
not want the body to limit the soul, we must master it and
control it through mortification. The spiritual life is an impossibility if the body is not mortified. Prayer certainly cannot be accompanied by self-indulgence. Saint Teresa insisted
that an explanation of prayer demands consideration of mortification. She intended to write about prayer, but added: "I
shall mention some things that are necessary for those who
seek to follow the way of prayer; so necessary that even if
these persons are not very contemplative, they can be far
advanced in the service of the Lord if they possess these
things. And if they do not possess them, it is impossible for
them to be very contemplative" (*W* 53). Contemplation is
a gift of God that He gives when He wills, as He wills, and
to whom He wills, and one may have to wait long before
receiving it; but if, meanwhile, we do what is indicated in
this chapter, we may be sure that we shall advance greatly in
perfection. If we are faithful, Our Lord will not fail us, but
it is we ourselves who must prepare in our souls the moral
atmosphere in which this grace can flourish.

~

Saint Teresa used three points to develop the second part
of her book: fraternal charity, detachment from all created
things, and true humility. This third point is really a section
in the discussion of detachment, for the Saint passes quickly

from detachment to humility, since the latter is also a form of detachment. But the first matter, fraternal charity, is developed separately.

In this plan, Saint Teresa has taught in practical language what Saint John of the Cross, her spiritual son and master, developed doctrinally in the first book of *The Ascent of Mount Carmel* (chap. 13): namely, that one does not arrive at the "all" except by passing through the "nothing". A true theologian, he not only explained it but proved it, basing himself on the nature of union: "In the state of divine union a man's will is so completely transformed in God's will that it excludes anything contrary to God's will, and in all and through all is motivated by the will of God."[1] To be united to God, then, one must have renounced self-love, since it is impossible to be united with God by love while self-love lurks in the soul. As long as there is the least attachment, transformation is not possible, for one will be motivated, not by divine love, but by self-love. The clear, unavoidable conclusion follows that every attachment must be renounced. A person of prayer who wishes to live not only for God but by God, moved truly in everything by the Holy Spirit, must cast out everything else, so he is moved only by the Holy Spirit. Saint Teresa taught that God will not give Himself completely unless the soul gives itself completely to Him. She does not prove her statement, but she is obviously convinced and wishes her followers to learn that one does not arrive at that state in which God communicates Himself to the soul except by means of a life of absolute generosity in the atmosphere of complete detachment.

[1] Saint John of the Cross, *Ascent of Mount Carmel*, bk. 1, chap. 11, no. 2, in *The Collected Works of St. John of the Cross*, trans. Kieran Kavanaugh, O.C.D., and Otilio Rodriguez, O.C.D. (Washington, D.C.: ICS Publications, Institute of Carmelite Studies, 1979), 96. Cf. also *The Spiritual Canticle*, stanza 37.

This second part of the *Way* actually takes us to the heart of the contemplative life. One does not attain depth in prayer unless he surrounds himself with mortification and detachment. This is the spiritual climate we must create in our soul if we wish our prayer to become contemplation.

Saint John of the Cross proved the absolute necessity of detachment by reasoning—setting up the principle and proving it. But principles are abstract. Saint Teresa viewed this teaching intuitively and went at once to its actual practice. She is both profound and psychologically sound; she not only stressed weak points but also indicated remedies, that is, how souls can be healed and made strong.

Purification of Love

"I shall enlarge on only three things. . . . The first of these is love for one another" (*W* 54). In this matter, Saint Teresa first discussed the purification of love and then, in chapter 7, explained the exercise of purified love.

First, let us glance at the psychology of love in human nature. Man has a single nature composed of soul and body, of spirit and matter. God made us thus, and we cannot change anything; we must sanctify ourselves as we are; our love is human love. We have a double power of love: we can love with the will and with the feelings; and we habitually do both, for we are one sole nature, one sole person. The will and the heart influence one another; these two powers of loving are often united, and we love with both the will and the feelings.

Both loves are guided by knowledge: sensible love by the senses, spiritual love by the intellect. Knowledge presents to us the object to love. Feeling responds to sensible knowledge, the will's inclination to intellectual knowledge. We love in a sensible way when we are drawn by external gifts, by a pleasing manner: a person with whom we get along well makes a sensible affection arise in our heart. If we think about this person, we nourish our sensible affection for him. And one can seek pleasure in the presence or the remembrance of the person loved; so this would be a less noble love, seeking satisfaction for oneself. The will's love, on the other hand, is nourished by the qualities that our intellect sees in others. Even in persons who make no appeal to our senses, our intellect can find reasons for love, and when it does, the will inclines to love.

Here lies the difference between sensible love and love of the will: the former can aim at one's own satisfaction, but the will's love—if the intention is kept pure—always thinks of the good of the other, even if it means forgetting oneself, renouncing one's own interests. This is noble love; the other could be much inferior.

Love of charity, or supernatural love, is spiritual, not sensible. God, to enable us to enter into His intimacy, has elevated our faculties with their acts to a supernatural order. The love He came to develop in us is spiritual, nourished by the intellect that considers what is lovable in persons—but the intellect is guided by faith, not merely the natural intellect.

We have seen that sensible love grows by seeing and communicating with the loved one; it can become self-centered and be nourished by the presence of a sensible good. Spiritual love, too, is moved by a good, but a good that the intellect, not the bodily eye, sees. This is love of charity guided by faith.

But that is not all: because man is a unit, a single person, there is mutual influence between the two forms of love. I feel within me these two urges to love, and I can love the same person with the will's love and with the affections. Often feeling is so strong that it tries to draw the will along with it. Though loving a person for his spiritual gifts, I may be captivated by his external qualities. I still love him spiritually, but my heart is no longer free. Now there is a passion of love; this is not a good thing. The will is superior to the feelings and should rule in us. If sensible love should come to dominate and draw the will after it, there would be a lack of balance that would do much harm.

But not only does feeling influence the will; the will's love also influences feeling: a blessed fact that allows God's grace to seize and elevate our whole being in prayer. Feeling, like intellect and will, is only one function of human psychic life, which makes us delight in the joys and suffer from the sorrows we meet on the way to union with God. If I love God with an active love of the will, feeling is easily awakened in me because of the harmony between the psychic functions.

The same thing that happens with love for God may happen toward creatures: there is nothing wrong or imperfect in this as long as feeling remains under control of the intellect and the will. So if I notice a sensible inclination toward a person whom I love spiritually, I will watch over my heart and not allow it to go beyond what God wills, loving in dependence on God and respecting the person according to the position in which God has placed him.

When there is question of loving God, to love Him with the feelings can help one love Him more with the will. But there is always danger of a little attachment to self, since such sentiments bring consolation and satisfy nature; thus God casts the soul into aridity to purify it.

~

After this review of the psychology of love, we can understand when Saint Teresa says: "It may seem that having excessive love among ourselves could not be evil, but such excess carries with it so much evil and so many imperfections that I don't think anyone will believe this save the one who has been an eyewitness. . . . Little by little it takes away the strength of will to be totally occupied in loving God" (*W* 54), because affection for creatures, when strong, becomes a passion and steals from the will the liberty of spirit necessary to love God with all one's power. Our affections need to be well disciplined. Our first parents, like us, had a double power of love, but they had also a special divine gift that harmonized spiritual and sensitive love in them. We cannot return to this perfect balance except by a firm discipline such as the one Teresa wished to indicate to her followers. To make us understand our need of it she lingered briefly upon a deviation from love, the particular friendship, indicated its inconveniences, insisted on the necessity of avoiding it, and gave remedies.

"I believe this excessive love must be found among women even more than among men" (*W* 54). Woman is more affectionate and therefore more prone to be ruled by sentiment and drawn by external attractiveness. But if her affection is well directed, it becomes a force to aid her in loving God. It spurs the will, and we see how strong love of God can be in a woman.

"But if the will should be inclined to one more than to another (this cannot be helped, for it is natural and we are often drawn to love the worst one if that person is endowed with more natural graces), let us be careful not to allow

ourselves to be dominated by that affection. Let us love the
virtues and interior good, and always studiously avoid paying attention to this exterior element" (*W* 55).

Perfect Love

Teresa resumed consideration of the theme of perfect love
in chapter 6. "Let us return now to the love that it is good
for us to have, that which I say is purely spiritual" (*W* 62).
How will she explain it to us? Had she been a theologian, she
would have defined it, but since she was not, she described
it. She lacked theological training, but she had theological
intuition; and if we glance at theology's definition, we shall
find all the characteristics she described.

Theologians define perfect spiritual love as a love that
seeks in God alone its entire foundation for its goodness.
For this reason, spiritual goods are sought for the soul. The
characteristics of this love are:

1. to seek its motive in God alone: love always has its
motives; the soul who loves purely loves with God as motive;

2. not to seek a return in any way: it is a love of pure
good will to give and is not concerned about receiving;

3. to desire spiritual goods for its beloved; if sometimes
it desires material goods for him, it is in view of spiritual
ones. And all supernatural goods are contained in the simple
desire that he be holy.

These are the characteristics of perfect love according to
the doctrine of Saint Thomas, and they correspond to those
given by Saint Teresa. The love of charity is that borne each
other by those who know how far God surpasses all creatures
and the place He deserves in our hearts and who therefore

cannot love except for His sake. They love because those they love belong to God. This is the sentiment of those who have given themselves completely to God. And it is the experience of how different from creatures God is that makes one give himself to God and never love anymore except for His sake.

How well the Saint spoke of this: "Those whom God brings to a certain clear knowledge . . . about the nature of the world . . . or about the nature of loving the Creator and loving the creature (and this seen through experience, which is entirely different from merely thinking about it or believing it)"—notice the reference to contemplative knowledge—"love very differently than do those who have not reached it" (*W* 62). Having given one's heart to God, one cannot give it to others and will not occupy himself with creatures except because God wills it. God wills us to love our neighbors, but only for their relation to Himself: they are His children. Therefore, we shall not love them for their natural gifts, for the pleasure of associating with them, but because "their God is our God."[2] And we shall love them with a love that knows by experience how different God is from everything created.

This is just what the world does not understand, not having experience of the transcendence of God. People today speak as if God should be at our service; but it is we who should be at the service of God: we are creatures dependent on Him. If today certain "mystiques" are arising that exalt the human personality, it is because awareness of God's transcendence is lacking. Man becomes the center of such false spirituality, and there is even a desire to make prayer serve him by putting at his disposal a force he lacks. But this

[2] Cf. Saint Augustine, *The City of God*, bk. 12.

is not serving God: it is loving oneself, subordinating God to man.

Saint Teresa understood well that, if we wish to love in a spiritual manner, God must occupy the central place in our life. Supernatural love is pure benevolence; sensible love desires its own satisfaction and, hence, is called by theologians "love of concupiscence".

"You will tell me that such perfect persons do not know how to love or repay the love others have for them—at least, they care little about being loved" (*W* 63). Persons who love spiritually do not really seek the satisfactions of the heart—those who do need a return of love. And what is the love of a creature compared to the love of God—eternal friendship? Whoever loves spiritually desires only help for the spiritual life and therefore seeks the good will of persons who can help him love God better; this is acting on a supernatural plane and is not seeking self-satisfaction, but looking to our end, which is God.

"When we desire love from some person, there is always a kind of seeking our own benefit or satisfaction" (*W* 63): this is not supernatural love. "It will seem to you that such [spiritual] persons do not love or know anyone but God. I say, yes they do love, with a much greater and more genuine love, and with passion, and with a more beneficial love; in short, it is love. And these souls are more inclined to give than to receive. Even with respect to the Creator Himself they want to give more than to receive" (*W* 64), because this love goes directly to God, desiring that our whole being should be consumed for His glory.

"You will also wonder what they have affection for if they do not love because of the things they see. It is true that what they see they love and what they hear they become attached to; but the things that they see are stable" (*W* 64).

They love what they see, but with the eyes of faith they see souls redeemed by Jesus Christ, with all the supernatural gifts for which they deserve love. And not living on the natural plane any longer, it would be out of place for them to desire anything that has only natural value; their desire is that others become perfectly pleasing to God.

In the last sentence of this chapter 6, the Saint proposes Jesus as model of fraternal love; Jesus gave Himself for souls, and we, loving our neighbor, must be ready to sacrifice ourselves for him and to show him all the delicacies of love we would show Jesus.

Exercise of Purified Love

Saint Teresa, treating of the exercise of pure spiritual love, placed it in opposition to natural love, which, though lawful, is imperfect and leads to weaknesses. Natural love is concerned with material goods and makes us anxious when the person we love has some misfortune; we are not at peace. Supernatural love is concerned only with spiritual goods: growth in grace and sanctity. Now we know it is not possible to become saints without trials; so we should know how to value the trials of those we love and, seeing them in the crucible of suffering, remember that God wishes to purify and sanctify them.

Still, as there is an interplay between the two forms of love, supernatural love cannot help feeling sympathy for its friends' sufferings. Even though one loves supernaturally and esteems suffering, one may also feel a first movement of resentment in these cases, but it will be controlled by the will, very different from a disordered and tyrannical affection. When we see someone who knows how to draw profit from his sufferings, we will rejoice, knowing the value of this great means of sanctity. In the encyclical *Mystici Corporis*, Pius XII exhorted the faithful during the terrible war years to draw profit from suffering: "We know that if all the sorrows and calamities of these stormy times, by which countless multitudes are being sorely tried, are accepted from God's hands with calm submission, they naturally lift souls above the passing things of earth to those of heaven that abide forever and arouse a certain secret thirst and intense desire for spiritual things. Thus, urged by the Holy Spirit, men are moved and, as it were, impelled to seek the kingdom of God with greater diligence." When we see someone suffering, we ought to pray that he put himself completely in God's hands, with the patience and courage needed to draw profit from trial.

Supernatural love, even when accompanied by a certain tenderness, does not look to anything but helping everyone to fulfill his duty well. One who loves both supernaturally and affectionately cannot allow his heart to be taken captive or do to others what is not right, just to please them; that would be weakness. Our love must not stoop to evil; it must sympathize with others and desire them to be perfect, without claiming a return of love.

II

Detachment

Saint Teresa stressed the importance of her second proposal in a rather striking manner: "Now let us talk about the detachment we ought to have, for detachment, if it is practiced with perfection, includes everything" (*W* 71).[1]

Of course, this does not mean that the practice of perfection is only an exercise of detachment. Detachment is a means, not an end; but it is a means that affects the whole spiritual life and, if practiced perfectly, leads one quickly to the goal. The Saint explains to us how this comes about: first, complete detachment does not constitute the exclusive means to sanctity, but, second, when a person is completely generous, God is generous to him and wills to bring him to divine union. Teresa merely states what Saint John of the Cross was later to write: "If a person is seeking God, his Beloved is seeking him much more."[2]

God seeks man by giving him more grace and the infused virtues that will make him beautiful, strong, and pleasing to

---

[1] Cf. the whole of chapter 8.
[2] Saint John of the Cross, *Living Flame of Love*, stanza 3, no. 28, in *The Collected Works of St. John of the Cross*, trans. Kieran Kavanaugh, O.C.D., and Otilio Rodriguez, O.C.D. (Washington, D.C.: ICS Publications, Institute of Carmelite Studies, 1979), 620.

Him. The virtues are like a cuirass that defends and strengthens, so that—when the gifts of the Holy Spirit make these virtues act more perfectly—a person grows in heroism and becomes capable of doing even the most difficult things for God. "If we embrace the Creator and care not at all for the whole of creation, His Majesty will infuse the virtues. Doing little by little what we can, we will have hardly anything else to fight against; it is the Lord who in our defense takes up the battle against the demons and against the world" (*W* 71).

With such an assurance, we can esteem the grace of complete detachment more sincerely: "of giving ourselves wholly to the All and keeping nothing for ourselves."

Self-Denial

Teresa employed the metaphor of a man who goes to bed quite peacefully, after bolting all his doors, although thieves are already in the house. "And you already know that there is no worse thief than we ourselves" (*W* 76). Our greatest enemy is self, our own person. Not that it is wrong to be a person. Mere "person" is taken in a pejorative sense, that is, the base personal tendencies we must combat, inclinations Saint Teresa called "self-will". "For if you do not walk very carefully and if each Sister is not alert in going against her own will as though doing so were more important than all else, there are many things that will take away this holy freedom of spirit by which you can fly to your Maker without being held down by clay or leaden feet" (*W* 76). Our souls are injured by the perverse qualities of our will. The "leaden feet" symbolize the useless—sometimes even injurious—preoccupations that a person brings upon himself if he holds to his own will (when he wants everything to go as *he* desires rather than as God wills). We need to remind ourselves that we seek a state of perfection wherein we lose our will in the will of God. As long as we cling to our will, we shall be burdened by "leaden feet", that is, preoccupations, and we shall lack freedom of spirit.

We must remember that *things* are not always bad: we can wish for good things, but in a selfish way. For instance, if we see a person doing something good, but not according to *our* way, we would almost like to force him to do it as *we* wish: yet there is no law that everything must go as we see it.

We must look higher, beyond our human ideas, even the best. God has His purposes, although most of the time His ways are mysterious to us. Despite our darkness and defects, He develops good in the souls of those who really want to love Him. The cause of our joy should be that God's plans are accomplished, not ours, even though ours are good. A person who conforms to the will of God is serene, seeing beyond secondary causes the first cause. We can have our desires, but our first desire should be to accept the divine will; so we should not be disturbed when we see our wishes unfulfilled.

This is what the Saint understands by self-will: the deliberate desire that things go according to personal taste. It can exist even in regard to virtues: for example, we plan to acquire humility and wish to do it in a month. Now, it is certain that God also wishes us to become humble, but He may permit us to exercise ourselves in this virtue without seeing the results. He wishes us to apply ourselves; we may be sure that we shall succeed, though perhaps not according to our plans.

~

As to means for detaching oneself, Teresa indicated those she used herself.

The first is to "bear in mind continually how all is vanity and how quickly everything comes to an end" (*W* 76). The world, immersed in temporalities, has lost its awareness of the transitoriness of created things. Many live as if they were going to live forever in this world. Perhaps we might not go this far, but we do tend to lose ourselves in details and attach far too much importance to details. Once we convince ourselves that everything passes and that what we desire may have little bearing on eternal life, we shall acquire true serenity.

The second means the Saint indicated is to turn to God when we find ourselves paying too much attention to something that interests us. Actually, the frustration we experience when we find that things do not succeed as we wish indicates our attachment to them. "The soul will be most careful in very little things. When we begin to become attached to something, we should strive to turn our thoughts from it and bring them back to God—and His Majesty helps" (*W* 76).

Regarding things that depend on circumstances not in our power, we are encouraged by Teresa to have an attitude of abandonment: "My God, think of us; I wish to think of You!" This is practically what Saint Teresa says to us. We want ourselves and everything we have to be His. When we find ourselves too preoccupied with something, we should repeat that we wish His (not our) plan to be carried out; He will help us to reach union with Him and to reach it as quickly as possible.

And, to facilitate self-denial, the Saint suggested a third means: humility. She gave only a few hints on it at this point; in another place she treated it more at length.[3]

"In finding these virtues [humility and mortification] you will find the manna. All things will taste good to you. However bad a thing may taste to those who are in the world, you will find it sweet" (*W* 77). This happens to one who has surrendered to the will of God. Saint Thérèse of the Child Jesus is a perfect example; by following the teaching of Saint John of the Cross,[4] she turned all her actions, even the most indifferent, into acts of love.

In general, Saint Teresa's remarks on detachment stress its necessity and the means for obtaining it; she extended an invitation to all to be generous with God in the practice of continual self-denial.

Interior Mortification

Teresa then proceeded to a discussion of interior mortification, which she called renouncement of the will, taking the word *will* in a rather broad sense to extend from one's natural inclinations to the occupations, persons, and objects in which he could find satisfaction.[5]

The Saint was aware that efforts at mortifying (or controlling) our spontaneous tendencies constitute a real "war against self". But she felt sure of God's help: "But once we

[3] We give the explanation of it with the comprehensive treatment of humility.

[4] Saint John of the Cross, *The Spiritual Canticle*, stanza 28, no. 8, in *Collected Works*, 522.

[5] The Saint treated of them extensively, devoting four chapters (12–15) to them, mentioning exercises of humility and of humiliation and teaching several in particular.

begin to work, God does so much in the soul and grants it so many favors that all that one can do in this life seems little" (*W* 81). It is another way of saying what we have already quoted from Saint John of the Cross: "If a person is seeking God, his Beloved is seeking him much more." Saint Thérèse of the Child Jesus often repeated this: "He made me *strong* and courageous, arming me with His weapons. Since that night I have never been defeated in any combat, but rather walked from victory to victory, beginning, so to speak, *'to run as a giant'*! . . . For a grace received faithfully, He granted me a multitude of others."[6] The quest of perfection indicates war against self, and that war is a costly one; yet a conviction that detachment is an essential means for reaching the fullness of divine life carries great power of motivation with it.

To attain complete generosity in detachment from self, Teresa offered several counsels. Her keen psychological intuition prompted her to say first that it is attained gradually: "This interior mortification is acquired, as I have said, by proceeding gradually, not giving in to our own will and appetites, even in little things, until the body is completely surrendered to the spirit" (*W* 82); and she speaks not only of our will, but also of our desire, that is, our natural inclinations. She continued to insist on this in the following paragraphs. "I repeat that the whole matter, or a great part of it, lies in losing concern about ourselves and our own satisfaction" (*W* 82); that is, not being anxious about them. Let us "try hard to go against our own will in everything. For if you are careful, as I said, you will gradually, without knowing how, find yourselves at the summit" (*W* 82).

---

[6] Saint Thérèse, *Story of a Soul*, trans. John Clarke, O.C.D., 3rd ed. (Washington, D.C.: ICS Publications, 1996), 97, 104.

Saint John of the Cross taught the same doctrine.[7] It frightens souls at first when they hear that they must be inclined "not to the easiest, but to the most difficult; . . . not to the consoling, but to the unconsoling; . . . not to wanting something, but to wanting nothing." He does not say simply that we must always *do* it; his teaching is still deeper: to be always *inclined* to do it, whenever possible. This is Teresa's doctrine: keep generosity alive and dynamic.

In concluding the subject of interior mortification, Saint Teresa anticipated an objection: "But how extremely rigorous, it seems, to say that we shouldn't please ourselves in anything" (*W* 82).

She had spoken of total detachment, practically a martyrdom. In answer, she insisted that detachment is not an end in itself but a means ordained to our sanctification for the glory of God.

---

[7] Saint John of the Cross, *Ascent of Mount Carmel*, bk. 1, chap. 13,, nos. 5–6, in *Collected Works*, 102–3.

III

Humility

Humility is the virtue that makes us stay *in our place* as creatures completely dependent upon God and anxious to do His will in everything. "This virtue and the virtue of detachment it seems to me always go together. They are two inseparable sisters. . . . You should embrace them and love them" (*W* 76–77). Teresa sought to win our love for these virtues, because we should love our littleness and desire to become like children. The child, conscious of its powerlessness, does not shrink within itself, but runs to its mother's arms; we should throw ourselves into God's arms and find the remedy for our weakness in His strength. Humility and trust are two aspects of the same virtue: without trust, humility would not be Christian, nor would it even be a virtue.

"These virtues [humility and mortification] have the characteristic of so hiding themselves from the person who possesses them that he never sees them or manages to believe that he has them even though he is told he does. But he esteems them so highly that he always goes about striving to obtain them, and he gradually perfects them within himself" (*W* 77). Those who sincerely seek humility can never feel that they possess it, because they are more conscious of their lack of it. Humility as an infused virtue cannot rule the soul completely until God puts it there; He does this by employing various types of humiliations. Humiliation is a hard and bitter bread, it is true, but very nourishing. Yet each humiliation accepted with love leads to greater love.

Avoiding Precedence

Saint Teresa described several practices of humility by way of advice toward attaining purity of soul, and the first of these is the struggle we must enter into against the desire to be preferred to others. She gave several examples of these desires, but the struggle in which we must engage is much wider than the few cases she mentioned.

"Take careful note of interior stirrings, especially if they have to do with privileges of rank" (*W* 83), and she described a few of these. But she wished her followers to go farther than repressing proud words: she urged them to combat the very thoughts that dictated them. The point in general is: we must avoid preferring ourselves to others.

Why are we prone to this defect? Because we are convinced that we are worth more, not in regard to everything, but in some specialized area. After finding that we have more capacity, we logically begin to wish others to agree; and we display our talent. Jesus did the contrary: He, the splendor of eternal light, hid Himself, let Himself be directed, above all in His infancy and at Nazareth; and in the years of the public life, He adapted Himself, infinitely superior as He was, to His apostles' imperfect way of acting.

The Saint next indicated the importance of vigilance in this matter for the contemplative life; where questions of honor reign, "You will never grow very much or come to enjoy the true fruit of prayer" (*W* 83). For Saint Teresa the fruit of prayer was intimate union with God, and both she and Saint John of the Cross insisted that this becomes a reality only after the soul practices absolute detachment. Thus, failure to mortify this inclination toward *the first place* constitutes a serious obstacle to intimacy with God. Realist that she was, Teresa admitted that sometimes God "gives consolations to those who are not so detached" (*W* 83), but then He makes an exception in order to help the soul, and He will not continue to favor it if it fails to correspond. Normally, therefore, only a person completely detached will reach contemplative union with God.

In chapter 3 of the "Fifth Dwelling Places" of the *Interior Castle*, the Saint wrote about the two forms of union that the soul can reach: union with the will of God and mystical union. Teresa held the former in higher esteem, since mystical union, after all, presupposes the other.

Saint John of the Cross affirmed the same:

> The third caution, directly against the devil, is that you ever seek with all your heart to humble yourself in word and in deed, rejoicing in the good of others as if it were your own, desiring that they be given precedence over you in all things; and this you should do wholeheartedly. You will thereby overcome evil with good, banish the devil, and possess a happy heart. Try to practice this more with those who least attract you. Realize that if you do not train yourself in this way, you will not attain real charity nor make any progress in it. Prefer to be taught by all rather than desire to teach even the least of all.[1]

---

[1] In the *Precautions*, Saint John of the Cross traced the foundation of the education of the contemplative; in the *Ascent of Mount Carmel*, he directed his conversation with God; and in *The Spiritual Canticle*, he described the whole spiritual road of the soul who seeks the goal of divine union. All three of these works were written for the Carmelite nuns of Beas and Granada.

We might ask why Saint John always makes the preparation for divine

~

Should detachment be lacking, even long years of "meditation" cannot lead to union with God. By "meditation" she here meant, not the main part of prayer—the intimate conversation with God, placing our will at His disposal—but the exercise of the reason. It is very possible for a person to practice meditation in this way for many years without its leading him to union with God; "imperfect prayer", she said, would bear greater fruit.

Mortification of every desire of precedence is an outstanding exercise of humility. Saint Teresa insisted on the close relationship between humility and the divine favors in many places in her works.[2] Every time she spoke of the dispositions for contemplation, she spoke of humility: "humility, and again humility". This actually is Christ's teaching, as shall soon become apparent.

Saint John of the Cross in the second book of the *Ascent* (chap. 7), said that when one can sincerely consider himself as nothing, he will have reached the state of union: "When he is brought to nothing, the highest degree of humility, the spiritual union between his soul and God will be effected."[3]

---

intimacy consist in detachment, while Saint Teresa stresses virtue. Actually virtue does detach the soul. The nine precautions of Saint John point out a whole program of detachment—one that can be put into practice by the exercise of the virtues.

[2] Cf. especially chapter 2 of the "Fourth Dwelling Places" in the *Interior Castle*.

[3] Saint John of the Cross, *Ascent of Mount Carmel*, bk. 2, chap. 7, no. 11, in *The Collected Works of St. John of the Cross*, trans. Kieran Kavanaugh, O.C.D., and Otilio Rodriguez, O.C.D. (Washington, D.C.: ICS Publications, Institute of Carmelite Studies, 1979), 125.

Saint Thérèse of the Child Jesus repeated the same doctrine when she spoke of the spiritual childhood that attracts Merciful Love. It is the teaching of the Gospel: "He has regarded the low estate of his handmaiden. . . . His mercy is on those who fear him." Jesus taught no doctrine more plainly than this: "He who humbles himself *will be exalted*." Note that the form of the first verb is active, that of the second, passive. God wishes man to realize that he cannot rely upon himself so that he may lean completely upon Him; then he shall be carried by Him to the heights of union with God.

~

After Teresa showed the importance of combatting sentiments of precedence, she counseled generosity and energy in the fight. "It doesn't seem to me the devil will tempt the truly humble person about rank even with the first stirrings. . . . He fears getting hurt" (*W* 84).

The devil is too astute to tempt a truly humble person, for the humble man uses the temptation to humble himself the more. "It is impossible for a person who is humble not to gain strength and progress in humility when the devil tempts him in this way" (*W* 84). When Saint Teresa Margaret was passing through the "night of the spirit", God made her see how little she corresponded with grace; yet (to us) she was so faithful! God does not lie: the light of contemplation shows clearly that God's invitations are far beyond our response to them.

Saint Teresa recommended careful study of the example of humility given by the Incarnate Word more than looking at our own misery—God's mercy, more than our defects.

This is the way to true interior humility and to the realization that our place, in all truth, is the last . . .

Along with interior humiliation, exterior humiliations are also encouraged as a means of conquering the temptation to preference and to turn it to our neighbor's profit. "Go about studying how to double your willingness to do things that go contrary to your nature. The Lord will reveal these things to you, and in this way and as a result the temptation will last only a short while" (*W* 84).

Effort is necessary, for "there is no toxin in the world that kills perfection" (*W* 84) like desiring honors. Saint Teresa ended with some reflections to emphasize what she said: "You will say that these are natural little things to which we need pay no attention" (*W* 84). Yes, certainly these are natural things, only too natural—completely opposed to the supernatural—and therefore worth greatly troubling about. "They increase like foam" (*W* 84).

Giving Up Our Rights

With chapter 13, Teresa began to discuss the second exercise of humility, which is the renunciation of our "little" rights. She gave the reasons for it, two models, and then other considerations to show how necessary it is.

"I have often told you, Sisters, and now I want to leave it in writing here so that you will not forget it, that in this house—and even in the case of any person seeking perfection—you should run a thousand miles from such expressions as 'I was right.' 'They had no reason for doing this to me.' 'The one who did this to me was wrong'" (*W* 85). This was not a mere passing thought or whim of the Saint, but a mature reflection she wished to leave in writing. It is closely bound to the first practice (of not seeking preference) and with the one that will follow (of not excusing oneself).

Saint Teresa felt that it was a serious imperfection to make such remarks. But if they are not spoken, much less should they be thought. A man's first reaction may be to feel hurt, but Teresa would have him not dwell on it, for to her it is "a right"—not always false in itself, but wrong in the sense that if he acts upon it he shall cease giving God everything.

This chapter 13 is a chain of arguments aimed at convincing the reader of the importance of this form of humility. "I don't know why the nun who doesn't want to carry the cross except the one that seems to her reasonable, is in the monastery" (*W* 85–86). How can anyone aspire to perfection if he accepts only merited crosses, while he rejects those that seem a little unjust?

But there is another motive: in no social group can all persons be treated with perfect justice. Everyone usually has to sacrifice some fraction of his rights. Human life is a whole network of mutual rights, and, because of man's limitations, not all of them are always going to be respected. If man had the intuitive intelligence of the angels, which sees everything in one glance, he could recognize all the needs and rights of others and remember them. Since man lacks this overall view, he easily forgets, with the result that another is hurt by lack of consideration.

Furthermore, each human being has a complete world within him that others cannot know, except by the limited outward expression of it that he wishes to give it. Thus it is ridiculous for us to fail to realize how little we know of others' needs and rights. All humanity is subject to this condition, and it is unreasonable to expect that one individual should be perfectly understood; we have to rise above these little things. There is no question of not having rights;

rather, it is a matter of not demanding them; we do not have to be always ready to fight for them.

This is the objective explanation behind this form of renunciation; there is also a subjective one. When man acts, he always has a valid explanation for it, but others do not always see it. Thus a man's conscience may tell him that he is right, whereas his neighbors might condemn him. Teresa remarked that this is the moment to renounce self-defense. In this way, she leads her reader toward her next counsel, which is not to excuse oneself.

Not Excusing Oneself

The third practice of humility that Saint Teresa suggested for creating a spiritual atmosphere favorable to contemplation consists in not excusing oneself. She wrote of it in the fifteenth chapter, outlining first in what it consists and then its motives.

She said that it is good to be silent when unjustly condemned, for this is great humility; she noted, however, that there are times when a man has to excuse himself to some degree. Once again Teresa exhibited her practicality: generosity always, but not exaggeration. She did not favor a man becoming a burden to others by the way in which he practiced virtue. Charity is the supreme virtue, and there are certain circumstances when silence might cause offense or scandal; someone may be disturbed, angered, hurt, or tempted thereby. But when discretion demands self-defense, man must temper it so that he does not lose completely the benefits of the humiliation.

Teresa herself left an example on the very day the first monastery of the Reform was founded. She was ordered to return at once to the monastery of the Incarnation to receive the censure of the Father Provincial. Her only thought was to imitate Jesus in His Passion by her silence.

> I went before him very happy to know I was suffering something for the Lord because in this case I didn't find I had committed any offense. . . . I recalled the judgment pronounced on Christ and saw how it amounted to nothing at all. I accused myself of the fault as one who was very much to blame, and this seemed true to anyone who didn't know all the reasons. After having received a serious reprimand, although not one as severe as the transgression deserved or in accordance with what many told the provincial, I didn't want to excuse myself; I had been determined about what I did. Rather, I begged to be pardoned and punished and that he not be vexed with me.
>
> I saw clearly that in some matters they condemned me without any fault on my part. . . . But in other matters I knew plainly they were speaking the truth, in saying that I was worse than others, in asking how, since I hadn't kept the strict religious observance of that house, I thought I could keep it in another stricter one, and in asserting that I gave scandal to the people and was promoting novelties. None of what they said caused me any disturbance or grief, although I let on that it did so as not to give the impression I didn't take to heart what they said to me. Finally the provincial ordered me to go before the nuns and give my account, and I had to do it.[4]

Such conduct brought her soul peace and sweetness, and God sustained her. When the time came for her to render the explanation demanded, neither Father Provincial nor the

[4] Saint Teresa of Jesus, *The Book of Her Life*, chap. 36, nos. 12–13, in vol. 1 of *The Collected Works of St. Teresa of Avila*, trans. Kieran Kavanaugh, O.C.D., and Otilio Rodriguez, O.C.D. (Washington, D.C.: ICS Publications, Institute of Carmelite Studies, 1976), 245.

nuns found anything for which to condemn her. When the nuns left, the superior spoke with her and was quite satisfied with the simple explanations she gave him; he even promised her permission to return to the new monastery as soon as the city had quieted down.

The second reason for not defending oneself flows from supernatural common sense. At times people will accuse a person of things that are not true, and he is unjustly corrected. But how many times does he err and no one notes it? Compensation is in order; besides, the Saint consoles her reader, it is better to be accused of faults one has not committed than to have really committed them.

Here Teresa burst into one of the beautiful exclamations that escaped her when she felt a thing deeply:

> O my Lord, when I think of the many ways You suffered and how You deserved none of these sufferings, I don't know what to say about myself, nor do I know where my common sense was when I didn't want to suffer, nor where I am when I excuse myself. You already know, my Good, that if I have some good it is a gift from no one else's hands but Yours. Now, Lord, what costs You more, to give much or little? If it is true that I have not merited this good, neither have I merited the favors You have granted me. Is it possible that I have wanted anyone to feel good about a thing as bad as I after so many evil things have been said about You who are the Good above all goods? Don't allow, don't allow, my God—nor would I ever want You to allow—that there be anything in Your servant that is displeasing in Your eyes. Observe, Lord, that mine are blind and satisfied with very little. Give me light and grant that I may truly desire to be abhorred by all since I have so often failed You who have loved me so faithfully.

What is this, my God? What do we expect to obtain from pleasing creatures? What does it matter if we are blamed a

lot by all of them if in Your presence we are without fault?
(*W* 92)

Liberty of Spirit

Finally, Saint Teresa described a great advantage of this practice. "For one begins to obtain freedom and doesn't care
whether they say good or evil of him but rather thinks of
what is said as though it were another's affair" (*W* 93). Man
obtains true inner solitude—more important than exterior
solitude—which places him alone with God without any
care except to please Him.

The person who, not from disdain, but for virtue's sake,
learns to remain serene and amiable when others judge ill of
him, grows constantly in interior solitude and the habit of
living with God. But one who pays attention to what others
think and say of him easily comes to act to win others' esteem. To be accused or reproved disturbs him. Not having
liberty of spirit, he has no interior solitude and wastes his
time in these useless considerations.

Whoever wants to act only for God will try not to be
concerned about the opinion of others. "This will seem
impossible to those of us who are very sensitive and little
mortified. In the beginning it is difficult; but I know that
such freedom, self-denial, and detachment from ourselves
can, with God's help, be attained" (*W* 93).

~

Later, in chapter 29, Teresa was to write of another phase
of this liberty of spirit: the phase wherein one does not
concern himself about the favor of superiors, about being

in their good graces. The habit is hard to acquire, but diligence in the quest for it will eventually obtain it.

What did Teresa mean by the "favor" (chap. 29) of superiors? She meant their showing, explicitly or implicitly, that they trust us and think highly of us. True, superiors owe goodwill to all alike, but they do not have to manifest it to all equally.

As natural satisfaction comes from finding that one's guides are pleased with us, it is a comfort needed by some. But it easily leads to self-seeking, to doing things well with the hidden desire to have them noticed, and so purity of intention is lost. Perhaps the person does not fall into sin at first, but he does stray away from the road of perfection, from seeking God alone; lacking this solace, he loses his tranquility. This is not perfection: "For the love of God, daughters, don't bother about being favored by lords or prelates" (*W* 145).

Of course, this does not mean one should be indifferent to the will of superiors and adapt the attitude "I act only for God and don't care about pleasing the superior." But it is our duty to please them by obeying them; then if they do not notice it, we ought not to torment ourselves. "Let each nun strive to do what she ought; if the bishop doesn't show gratitude for what she does, she can be sure that the Lord will repay and be grateful for it" (*W* 145–46).

Since anxiety about superiors' favor could harm souls, the Saint gave two remedies:—

1. *To remember that all things are passing.* "Let us always direct our thoughts to what is lasting and pay no attention to things here below, for even though our lives are short these preferences do not last for us" (*W* 146). And among these earthly things there is the pleasure stemming from the approval of superiors. "Give no room to these thoughts. . . .

Cut them off with the thought that your kingdom is not here below and of how quickly all things come to an end" (*W* 146). This is a sort of philosophical consolation: everything is passing, so let us not pay too much attention to it— a good and effective means, but not the most perfect, even though it be used with a supernatural viewpoint. "But even this kind of remedy is a lowly one and not indicative of great perfection" (*W* 146).

2. *To love humiliation.* There certainly is a little humiliation in doing all one can and then not receiving the esteem one might merit. Yet to have this happen does not surprise one who knows human nature; it follows upon human limitation. In judging persons, we are influenced by secondary things and often do not notice essentials; hence, our judgment is incomplete. We look more readily at the negative side than at the positive, because defects are more obvious.

And this applies, not only to the attitude of superiors toward us, but also to that of all those who surround us. It is a satisfaction to feel about us a certain esteem, not manifested in words, but in so many little ways . . .

Saint Teresa counseled her followers not to desire an escape from this state of humiliation—rather desire that it should continue, persuaded that one does not reach deep humility without humiliation.

"It is better that this disfavor of your superior continue, that you be unappreciated and humbled, and that you accept this for the Lord who is with you. Turn your eyes inward and look within yourself, as has been said. You will find your Master, for He will not fail you; rather, the less you have of exterior consolation the more He will favor you" (*W* 146).

IV

Conclusion of the Second Part

The sixteenth chapter concludes the foundation section of the *Way of Perfection*. It summarizes Teresian thought on the virtues and links it with the following chapters, which study prayer's contribution toward the possession of contemplation.

The first four paragraphs are in the first (but not in the second) manuscript of the *Way*. Saint Teresa suppressed them in the latter, which still exists and shows that five pages have been torn out and replaced by only one, wherein the Saint probably summarized the thought of the suppressed pages. We cannot be absolutely certain of this, but everything indicates that these five pages must have been substantially the same as those in the Escorial manuscript giving the comparison of the game of chess. She must have deleted this example out of delicacy toward her daughters, to whom she forbade games. But she retained the idea, which is very important.

Thus we have the fifth paragraph written to replace the preceding ones. Editors, however, have generally restored the first four, for the comparison was very expressive.

There are three points in this chapter: first, the need of virtues to arrive at contemplation; second, the exceptions God is pleased to make at times—but they are *exceptions* that only confirm the rule; and third, a statement of her plan to treat of contemplation; thus, this chapter serves as a transit to the following part.

In the first part of the *Way of Perfection*, Teresa insisted again and again on sincere generosity in the practice of the virtues. Once again, at this point, she repeated this teaching: "Don't think that what I have said so far is all I have to say" (*W* 93). Like the chess player, she has done no more than set out the pieces. In this game, the object is to take "the king"; but first must come the placing of the pieces, the chief of which is "the queen"; then follows skillful maneuvering, especially of the "queen", who has great power over the king. In other words, Saint Teresa remarked that up to this point her book has been merely a placing of the pieces, but now it is time to move them; that is, it does not suffice to form great plans of virtue; we also have to apply ourselves.

"The queen is the piece that can carry on the best battle in this game, and all the other pieces help. There's no queen like humility for making the King surrender. Humility drew the King from heaven to the womb of the Virgin, and with it, by one hair, we will draw Him to our souls. And realize that the one who has more humility will be the one who possesses Him more; and the one who has less will possess Him less" (*W* 94).

Why this pressing invitation to practice humility? If it were only meditation, certainly all this would not be necessary as foundation, because meditation itself should help in the practice of virtue. But the goal is contemplation.

"Had you asked about meditation I could have spoken about it and counseled all to practice it even though they do not possess the virtues, for meditation is the basis for acquiring all the virtues. . . . But contemplation is something else, daughters . . . for this King doesn't give Himself but to those who give themselves entirely to Him" (*W* 94–95). Here, then, is the reason for asking so much: the soul surrenders to God only by the generous exercise of virtue, and only in this way will it succeed in conquering the King, that is, in being introduced into His intimacy, into holy contemplation. It is the same thought we read farther back: He "does not give Himself wholly until we are giving ourselves wholly to Him"; and we can now understand the remark with reference to contemplation.

In the fifth paragraph, which was to have taken the place of the first four, which she suppressed, this idea is repeated. ("Mental prayer" is here used in the sense of "meditation".) "Therefore, daughters, if you desire that I tell you about the way that leads to contemplation, you will have to bear with me if I enlarge a little on some other matters even though they may not seem to you so important; for in my opinion they are. And if you don't want to hear about them or put them into practice, stay with your mental prayer for your whole life" (*W* 95).

And because she has spoken so decidedly, a thought drawn from her own experience here presented itself to her: it can happen that God does not wait for the soul to be generous to give it this gift. But we must not misunderstand her: this does not happen normally, but only by an act of mercy. It is an exception that confirms the rule, because if this soul is not truly faithful, what God has given it will not last. "There are times when God will want to grant some great favor to persons who are in a bad state so as to draw them by this means out of the hands of the devil" (*W* 95).

This expression, "bad state", has raised a discussion among theologians. Some have thought there was question of mortal sin, from which God would make the soul rise by means of a contemplative grace. But comparing the two manuscripts of the Escorial and of Valladolid shows that such was not the Saint's thought. One not in the grace of God can receive a grace "gratis data" (for example, a vision) but not contemplation, which is the fruit of the development of grace in the soul. Father John of Jesus and Mary, O.C.D., said that this grace "gratis data" would actually be a grace of conversion.[1] In fact, some think this was the case with Saint Paul, though it is not known whether he really was in a state of serious sin. However, Saint Teresa was referring to the state of tepidity or little fervor.

God, then, comes to solicit this soul; if the individual does not correspond, God will not continue His favors and the individual will not advance. But if he is faithful, God will not stop until He has carried him very high: He will make him progress to the state of contemplative union with Him. He will be among His "beloved children".

> For myself I hold that there are many to whom our Lord God gives this test, but few who prepare themselves for the enjoyment of the favor of contemplation. When the Lord grants it and we do not fail on our part, I hold as certain that He never ceases to give until we reach a very high degree. When we do not give ourselves to His Majesty with the determination with which He gives Himself to us, He does a good deal by leaving us in mental prayer and visiting us from time to time like servants in His vineyard. But these others are favored children. He would not want them to leave His side, nor does He leave them, for they no longer want to leave Him. He seats them at His table, He shares with them His food even to the point of taking a portion from His own mouth to give them. (*W* 96–97)

[1] Cf. Joannes a Jesu Maria, O.C.D., *Theologia mystica*, chap. 3 (Freiburg, 1912), 38–39.

She concluded the chapter by a call to renewed fervor. Let her follower concentrate on the way of contemplation that is that of the perfect life, of intense virtue. This involves the intellect first, which should keep its attention fixed upon this way. Then the will must play its part: before a particularly demanding act of virtue let us never say, to excuse ourselves, that we are not saints. If God asks generous virtue of us, it is to help us to become saints; His grace will never fail us.

Here she made another allusion to the practice of humility, about which she spoke in the preceding chapters: "Any slight loss in one's honor is not tolerated. . . . God deliver us, Sisters, when we do something imperfect, from saying: 'We're not angels, we're not saints.' Consider that even though we're not, it is a great good to think that if we try we can become saints with God's help. And have no fear that He will fail if we don't fail" (*W* 98).

Then Teresa announced the theme that was to begin with chapter 17: an explanation of the nature of mental prayer and contemplation. And here ends the ascetical part of the *Way of Perfection*.

PART III

THE FOUNT OF
LIVING WATER

I

Dispositions

The works of Saint Teresa are all treatises on prayer. If in the *Way of Perfection* she spoke at such length about the virtues, it was because these are the foundation for prayer and prepare the spiritual climate in which it can become contemplative.

Saint Teresa was undoubtedly a great writer, but her works abound in digressions. From one point of view, this is a fault, but it adds force and completeness to her expression. Her disciple soon perceives that these digressions do not hinder the development of the thought; actually, once she ended the digression, she resumed the train of thought that had seemed lost.

This style shows itself especially in her *Way*; although there is a logical order, she continually anticipated what she wished to say later. She would have liked to tell everything about the life of prayer all at once. She was eager to have her readers put their hearts into their mental prayer, so that it might later become contemplative.

But what is the order in this part of her book? There are two main points: first, the soul's attitude toward the gift of contemplation; second, two principles in regard to contemplation.

First, then, the right attitude toward this divine gift; Teresa knew that the treatment of this matter was a very delicate matter. On the one hand, contemplation is a free gift that God gives to whom He wills, when He wills, as He wills, and, on the other hand, there is question of our attitude toward it. We must think of it *humbly*, not thinking we have a right to contemplation (chap. 17), with *generosity* (chap. 18), with *lively desire* (chap. 19), and with *complete resignation* (chap. 20). These are important chapters, which, while they describe the individual's attitude toward contemplation, anticipate many ideas about the life of prayer that Teresa treated in more detail later.

Then (the second point we mentioned above), the Saint taught two principles that she had already stated; but, from the middle of chapter 20, she began to treat them more explicitly, continuing till the end of chapter twenty-five. These are: (1) the life of prayer requires effort, and (2) the prayer must be mental prayer.

With regard to the effort: one should be resolved to consecrate his whole life to it, for it is a way (that of prayer) on which he must travel and continue to travel until he reaches the end. She suggested solutions to various hindrances: impossibility, health, and so on. If one is not capable of methodical meditation, it does not matter: there are other ways of making mental prayer. She would show what the essence of prayer is when freed from accessories: namely, elevation of the mind to God, touching Him with our intellect and will. She would say: yes, recite your vocal prayers, but that is not enough; you must understand to Whom you speak, and who you are who speak: the Creator and the creature, the Father and the son; and then also know the Teacher, the blessed Jesus, and what He teaches. One who learns to think of this makes mental prayer even while he recites his vocal prayers. And only mental prayer leads to contemplation.

Resignation

A man must not think he has a right to contemplation. A truly humble person makes no claim to it. Teresa had insisted so much in the preceding chapters on showing that contemplation develops in an environment where virtue flourishes; she now asked: "How could a truly humble person think he is as good as those who are contemplatives?" (*W*98–99). No one should expect contemplation before reaching heroic virtue, and no one ought to believe he has reached heroic virtue, especially heroic humility. Saint Teresa was of the opinion that we should never believe our virtue so firmly established that we could claim the gift of contemplation as a reward.

Yet, while the person applies himself diligently to the practice of virtue, he must not abandon his desire for contemplation. But if God is not pleased to grant him contemplation, he should not become downcast; there are many ways of serving God. We ought never to renounce hope of contemplation, but neither ought we to demand it at once: we need to know how to wait, surrendering ourselves to God. This is the way to receive His graces.

But why did Saint Teresa insist so much on these thoughts? First of all, because contemplation is a gift and not a right; then, because the ways of God are many and different, and God does not conduct all souls—not even two, says Saint John of the Cross[1]—by the same way. God gives this gift

---

[1] Saint John of the Cross, *Living Flame of Love*, stanza 3, no. 59, in *The*

according to His good pleasure. The practice of virtue leads to sanctity, which is much more important than contemplation; contemplation is only a means to sanctity; sanctity is the goal. It is true that the center of the spiritual life is love and that contemplation is a great aid in reaching perfect love; still, it is only a means.

Even those whom God does not conduct by the way of contemplation should do as the others, that is, prepare themselves, because no one knows when God wishes to give this gift. Sometimes it comes very late. Teresa cited her own case as an example: "I spent fourteen years never being able to practice meditation without reading" (*W* 99). So she was far from being immersed in contemplation, and "there will be many persons of this sort" (*W* 99).

And there are those who cannot even meditate, but have just to go gleaning here and there in their books, as Saint Thérèse did. There are others who cannot even do this, "but [are] able only to pray vocally, and in this vocal prayer they will spend most of their time" (*W* 99). Teresa felt great pity for these restless spirits who can never concentrate; later she was to show them how to make vocal prayer in a way that might lead them to contemplation. She mentioned the example of an old woman she knew: "I know an elderly person who lives a good life, is penitential and an excellent servant of God, who has spent many hours for many years in vocal prayer, but in mental prayer she's helpless; the most she can do is go slowly in reciting the vocal prayers. There are a number of other persons of this kind" (*W* 99–100);

Collected Works of St. John of the Cross, trans. Kieran Kavanaugh, O.C.D., and Otilio Rodriguez, O.C.D. (Washington, D.C.: ICS Publications, Institute of Carmelite Studies, 1979), 633.

she even knew of persons consecrated to the life of prayer who do not go any farther than this. "I don't believe they will be any the worse off in the end . . . and in a way they will be more secure, for we do not know if the delights are from God or from the devil" (*W* 100).

She also gave the example of Saint Martha, who "was a saint, even though they do not say she was contemplative" (*W* 100). As to the possibility of reaching perfection, she saw no difference between the two classes; she had just said, "Don't be afraid that you will fail to reach the perfection of those who are very contemplative" (*W* 100). If Saint Martha "had been enraptured like the Magdalene, there wouldn't have been anyone to give food to the divine Guest" (*W* 100).

It might be one's own fault that he does not attain contemplation; he might have been unfaithful. But we never know for certain, since it remains God's own gift. "Be sure that if you do what lies in your power, preparing yourselves for contemplation with the perfection mentioned, and that if He doesn't give it to you (and I believe He will give it if detachment and humility are truly present), He will save this gift for you so as to grant it to you all at once in heaven" (*W* 101). She was convinced that God would give it; if not in its fullness, at least a little.

Teresa ended the discussion by repeating that the choice is not left to us. All would have chosen contemplation, thinking thus to enjoy greater repose and consolation. No one should think he has any claim to contemplation; he should prepare himself, for otherwise he might not be ready for the divine invitation. If he prepares himself well and yet has to wait, God will know how to recompense him generously in the other life. Teresa felt certain, however, that God would grant a sincere man some form of contemplation, perhaps only briefly.

Contemplation and Suffering

Man's attitude toward God's free gift of contemplation should be one of humble abandonment and great generosity. Generosity in being faithful to prayer, yes, but also in preparing the proper atmosphere or climate for it.

Saint Teresa wrote about this atmosphere of contemplation: "Those who do walk along [this path] . . . do not bear a lighter cross; and you would be surprised at the ways and modes in which God gives them crosses. . . . I know clearly that the trials God gives to contemplatives are intolerable" (*W* 102). Those who have not received contemplative graces may find a motive of humility in these thoughts, thinking that, if they do not receive such graces, it is because they might not yet be capable of suffering so much and therefore God holds back.

But this introduction is merely a pretext to introduce a very important truth: a person who wishes to reach contemplation must be willing to suffer. The sufferings of contemplatives are always great. This can be a consolation in a way, because one can think: I should not be able to bear them. But that is true only up to a certain point, because a loving soul will always think, "God can strengthen me." One can always ask Him to do that.

A contemplative enters into God's intimacy and knows intuitively that Jesus always draws one He unites to Himself by the way of the cross: a spouse cannot do less than follow the lot of his Spouse; sharing His life, he will fill up what is lacking in His Passion. Jesus counts on him to participate in His sufferings and in His redemptive work.

There is no necessity to feel delight in suffering or to attempt forcing oneself to have this feeling; the spiritual life does not rest on feeling, but on the will with which we accept the suffering God sends us. An acute physical or spiritual suffering does not mean anything if it does not cost us anything, but if it costs, it is precious before God, because then we give Him most. Jesus suffered thus, even to the point of saying: "My soul is very sorrowful, even to death" (Mt 26:38). "To suffer with joy", said Saint Thérèse, "does not mean to suffer with delight, but with serenity, with complete abandonment." How many times had she reached the depth and felt she could do no more! But that did not matter, for she gave all her strength, and it was then that Jesus came to her rescue.

Here Saint Teresa anticipated a thought to which she would return more in detail when she commented on the *Pater noster*, at the words "Fiat voluntas tua" (*W* 160). "Since God wants to lead those whom He greatly loves by the path of tribulation—and the more He loves them the greater the tribulation . . ." (*W* 102). Certainly, when God calls a person to His intimacy by means of an abundance of contemplative graces, that person should expect to be introduced into the way of the cross, also; that is one of the signs that God loves him.

And now that she had shown what generosity it takes to prepare for contemplation, Saint Teresa returned (fourth paragraph) to the idea that we should *all* prepare ourselves. She realized that temperaments differ; and so do manners of making mental prayer. Though she used the words "vocal prayer", it is certainly not a mere recital of them that she recommended. She also mentioned meditative reading and conversations with God: all different ways of devoting the set time to prayer.

Anyone who is not faithful to this set time misses an appointment, as it were, and runs the risk of arriving after the door is closed and thus losing God's graces. God has His hours, and if a person does not keep his engagement with Him, he feels the consequences in his spiritual life.

Responsibility of Contemplatives

Saint Teresa explained that a contemplative should be willing to suffer; now she returned to the responsibility such a one has in the Church (chap. 18, *W* 103-4). We know from the dogma of the communion of saints that everyone has some responsibility, and those explicitly called to help the Church have the greater duty in this regard. Contemplatives should not forget that the more abundant contemplative grace is, the more generous they ought to be. If God, by means of contemplation, calls a person to intimacy with Himself, He is calling him to share in Jesus' life and, consequently, to help on the way of the cross. So a contemplative must be generous, or he will disappoint God.

God's interests are vast, and a person of prayer should be continually occupied with them. For them God asks the daily sufferings that are sometimes so heavy because of their persistence. It is not easy to be always serene and joyous, remembering that all this is willed by God for our good, nourishing our apostolic ideal with continual immolation, making no reserves in this crucifying life. And if sometimes God allows the suffering to go to the limit of our strength, all our power will come from Him. When He asks more of us, He will also help us more.

~

Toward the end of this chapter (18), Teresa again wrote about what one can do to prepare himself for contemplation. The first time, it was prayer she emphasized; now it is virtue. Again she repeated that the soul's progress consists much more in the virtues than in contemplative graces, helpful though the latter are. This is true progress: if contemplation has any importance, it is because it makes the soul more generous.

In naming the virtues, she tarried a moment on obedience, but then remarked that the nuns to whom she was writing already knew this virtue very well, and so she would not enlarge upon it. She wrote of it at greater length in the fifth chapter of the *Foundations*.

Let us conclude with Saint Teresa by saying that the preparation for contemplation should be very fervent. We should cultivate a contemplative mentality, that is, a spirit of generosity, so that we can really welcome suffering—in the concrete.

II

The Living Water

Saint Teresa praised a lively desire for contemplation; in chapter 19, she set out to show how one can dispose himself for it in actual practice. She considered it a proximate goal toward which we should tend.

The Saint had a tendency to return time and again to topics that she felt to be of utmost importance. Hence at the beginning of chapter 19, after a long digression, she could not remember what point she had reached and did not want to lose time rereading what she had already written, so she spoke anew of the need to apply oneself to mental prayer. As a good teacher, she realized that not all individuals are alike and that each must discover for himself the way God desires him to follow.

Teresa began with the most normal case—though it may not be the most frequent—which is that of those who can follow a determined method in meditation. In Saint Teresa's time, various writers had already written books suitable for meditation.

Besides the Exercises of Saint Ignatius (containing the method for meditation, not the application), there were the books by Luis de Granada, the Dominican, and Saint Peter of Alcantara, the Franciscan. Saint Teresa knew these books and recommended them and even referred to those of Luis de Granada when she wrote in this chapter 19: "There are books in which the mysteries of the Lord's life and Passion are divided according to the days of the week, and there are meditations about judgment, hell, our nothingness, and the many things we owe God together with excellent doctrine and method concerning the beginning and end of prayer" (*W* 106). Anyone who travels by such a good road, she said, would be brought by God "to the haven of light. And through such a good beginning the end will be reached" (*W* 106).

So there is no doubt that the Saint approved of methods in meditation. "All who are able to walk along this path will have rest and security, for when the intellect is bound one proceeds peacefully" (*W* 106), that is, when the intellect remains on a subject and studies it, thus avoiding distractions and reaching good resolutions. Certainly a soul who has facility in doing this is well disposed for contemplation and has only to practice the self-denial so much recommended by the Saint throughout the entire second part of the *Way*.

Difficulties

Yet Teresa observed that not all are capable of methodical meditation. She did not, however, dispense them from mental prayer; perhaps they cannot make it in a methodical manner, but they can make it equally well—and it is precisely of this she wrote in the part of the *Way* that remains for us to explain. She sought to come to their aid and teach them how to prepare themselves for contemplation and intimacy with God.

"There are some souls and minds so scattered they are like wild horses no one can stop. Now they're running here, now there, always restless. . . . This restlessness is either caused by the soul's nature or permitted by God" (*W* 107). They are tormented by distractions; it is difficult for them to concentrate. Saint Teresa was not alarmed and did not say that they cannot reach contemplation on that account; but they do have to follow another method to make their prayer. "I pity these souls greatly", said the Saint (*W* 107).

Their difficulty may come from a natural defect or from passing circumstances that God permits to make their minds wander. Saint Thérèse, for example, experienced distractions because the drowsiness she suffered made it hard for her to concentrate. Saint John of the Cross speaks of still another cause when treating of contemplation with indistinct and loving attention; he notes that in those whom God draws to this kind of prayer, a certain movement of the imagination remains and makes prayer wearisome at times. In all these cases, we should try to help ourselves, but not always in the same way.

Reading is one of the ways Teresa mentioned in the last chapter. She was to show later that she did not wish us to resort to a book in every moment of aridity, even though it is accompanied by distractions; for at times God wishes us to have patience and stay there in silence in His presence, desiring Him.

But when some natural circumstance, physical or psychical, causes the dryness, then is the time she counseled recourse to a book. This is when Saint Thérèse used one. Though it did not always remedy matters, still we know from her writings that many a time, after she had faithfully tried to help herself through her prayer time with a book and still remained dry, at the end she received light leading her ever farther along that "little way" of hers which she was later to show others.

> It happens that after [some] have conquered the first enemy through their labor—and through a great deal of labor—they let themselves be conquered by the second; they would rather die of thirst than drink water so costly. Their efforts cease, their courage fails. And when some have the courage to conquer the second class of enemy as well, their strength gives way when they meet the third, and perhaps they were no more than two steps from the fount of living water, of which the Savior said to the Samaritan woman, "whoever drinks of it will never thirst." (*W* 107)

Contemplation

The beautiful incident of the Samaritan woman recalled to Teresa what she had promised her daughters to write about. For her the living water was contemplation. When she wrote, she aimed at awakening in her reader a desire for it. Coupled with this desire, Teresa added fidelity to the practice of mental prayer and the exercise of the virtues.

"Such a person will not thirst for anything in this life—although thirst for the things of the next life increases much more than can ever be imagined through natural thirst" (*W* 107). Here again is the Saint's fundamental thought: contemplation is a great help to turn a person totally toward God. Great souls grasp the truth that only God can satisfy man, so that there is nothing else to be done but to go on toward Him and so that whoever does not reach Him will be unhappy forever. Human life is a road to God, a continual traveling toward Him. Contemplation is a powerful assistance on the journey, for it gathers up all one's energies and turns them toward God; one no longer thirsts for other things, but only to please God.

But note: contemplation is not perfection. For Saint Teresa, perfection is always the perfection of love, expressed by adhering to God's will. But contemplation helps immensely to put us in this disposition, and that is why she felt forced to speak of it. She continued Our Lord's metaphor of the "living water"; thinking of the benefits of water in the natural order, she went on to consider the same qualities in the supernatural order. She would speak of that ineffable water which is contemplation and, in particular, of three of its properties. (She considered it in its fullness: unitive contemplation.[1] Not all contemplation is unitive; there are different grades in which such properties are met in lesser measure.)

What are these qualities?

Water cools, cleanses, and quenches thirst.

~

Water cools: the spiritual water of contemplation cools and slakes thirst for earthly things, leaving a man longing only for those of heaven; it refreshes by making detachment easier.

Contemplation that has become unitive supposes that a person has attained a certain perfection in virtue, especially charity. Sometimes God does give this grace to an imperfect individual, but normally it supposes a strong love, full conformity of one's own will with that of God. Teresa enlarged

[1] That she intends to speak of unitive contemplation is stated explicitly in paragraph 6: "This water . . . this divine union is something very supernatural" (*W* 109).

this comparison with natural water by adding what happens when water is thrown on a pitch or tar fire: the flames grow fiercer. Now, when a soul receives unitive contemplation, it is already strong in love, and the water of contemplation makes the fire of its love burn the more, because these two have the same origin: the love of charity infused by God into the soul.

Theologically speaking, the prayer of union supposes that God strongly attracts the individual's love. When a soul is already burning with love stemming from its own initiative, it burns much more when God attracts it, as He does through unitive contemplation. Thus it becomes a great aid to carry souls toward God: it reinvigorates them before temptations and the attractions of creatures. If man's whole life is nothing but a search for God, the paramount importance of this grace becomes quite obvious.

Here Teresa made reference to the tears of love for God that are sometimes shed in this prayer. These, too, come from God, yet they are not that living water which kindles the fire of love; rather, they flow from it.

~

Water cleanses: the second property of perfect contemplation is to cleanse. Union with God is impossible without perfect purity of soul. The water of contemplation purifies, removes the dross, and makes the soul more pleasing to God. Here again the Saint spoke of unitive contemplation and, recalling her personal experience, hinted at what she narrated in the book of her *Life*,[2] which actually is the story of all

---

[2] Cf. Saint Teresa of Jesus, *The Book of Her Life*, chap. 36, no. 6, in vol. 1

souls. After having struggled for a long time against a defect without succeeding in freeing herself from it, Teresa was freed from it in a moment when God gave her the prayer of union. It is always thus: God wishes that man exert himself; finally, He will come and raise him Himself.

Perfect contemplation is a powerful means to detachment and purification; but not unitive contemplation only, for the lesser degrees also have this cleansing force, though in minor and progressive grades, as Saint John of the Cross has said. He insisted strongly on this purifying character of contemplation; and there is no better exposition of it than his pages on the night of sense in which, by means of purifying graces, God prepares the soul for initial contemplation and then, by very severe trials, for unitive contemplation. Even the latter does not lose the purifying quality proper to contemplation, though it has this quality in a minor degree.

Here, then, is a new phase of contemplation, one that should make it desirable, not for the enjoyment flowing from it, but for the help it gives to enter more fully into the life of love. The aim of perfection is love; the purpose of the contemplative life, as has been said, is to help toward this aim.

To make us understand better how contemplative grace purifies, Saint Teresa made a comparison between meditation and contemplation. In meditation, recollections of worldly concern may intrude on our reasonings, and, if we are not on the alert, our attention may wander. In the prayer of union, this danger does not exist, for the contemplative grace, proper to this prayer, prevents the soul from being

---

of *The Collected Works of St. Teresa of Avila*, trans. Kieran Kavanaugh, O.C.D., and Otilio Rodriguez, O.C.D. (Washington, D.C.: ICS Publications, Institute of Carmelite Studies, 1976), 161.

distracted. Even in the lower forms of contemplation, this property is verified, though in a minor way; in the prayer of quiet, the soul can still be distracted but, as it feels God drawing it, it finds it easy to remain with Him.

~

The third property of water is that it quenches thirst. But the water of contemplation, instead of taking away thirst, increases man's thirst for the things of God. A taste of this water kindles such great thirst that one cannot think of anything else except to taste God more. Then follows a powerful orientation toward God: all the soul's energies turn to Him. Contemplation is not desired for the pleasure it gives, but it is a fact that this pleasure does help orient one toward Him. In contemplation, man tastes his God—even though it may be only a little—and this distant participation in heavenly beatitude greatly arouses his hope. And hope stimulates the exercise of love.

Here the Saint observed that the desire of heaven, which the soul carries away from unitive contemplation, can be influenced by natural sensitivity. This influence should be moderated. The mystical Doctor, Saint John of the Cross, says in the *Flame*[3] that in persons who have reached the spiritual marriage, this desire is totally abandoned to the will of God, because harmony is complete: nature is completely subject and cannot disturb the spirit any longer. We can gather from her sixth *Relation* that when Saint Teresa was

---

[3] Saint John of the Cross, *Living Flame of Love*, stanza 1, no. 23, in *The Collected Works of St. John of the Cross*, trans. Kieran Kavanaugh, O.C.D., and Otilio Rodriguez, O.C.D. (Washington, D.C.: ICS Publications, Institute of Carmelite Studies, 1979), 588–89.

near the end of her life, her soul experienced complete resignation to God. But in the espousals this is not the case, and nature, which always seeks its enjoyment, may enter into this desire for God. In the impulses that one may feel, he ought not believe that everything is perfect; vigilance and control are always necessary. It is simply a matter of common sense, confirmed by theology.

Thus contemplation is a very desirable gift, not so much because it causes one to enjoy God, but because it is a strong incentive along the way of love. Contemplation quickens the most sublime love, that of benevolence; it makes man solicitous for God's interests.

The Divine Invitation

"Why do you think, daughters, that I have tried to explain the goal and show you the reward before the battle, by telling you about the good that comes from drinking of this heavenly fount, of this living water?" (*W* 113).

The "goal" she spoke of is contemplation, the crown bestowed on the struggle. And she told us "about the good that comes from drinking of this heavenly fount, of this living water" by considering how contemplation detaches one more and more from the world and orients him ever more toward God, concentrating his heart in God.

"[I have done so] so that you will not be dismayed by the trial and contradiction there is along the way, and advance with courage and not grow weary. For . . . it can happen that after having arrived you will have nothing left to do but stoop and drink from the fount; and yet you will abandon everything and lose this good, thinking that you have not the strength to reach it and that you are not meant for it" (*W* 113).

If the call to contemplation were not for everyone, one might ask himself: "Am I among these privileged souls?" And an apparent humility might make him answer: "But it is such a sublime thing!" Everyone is invited to sanctity, and the Saint added very energetically that everyone is invited to contemplation, also.

"If this invitation were not a general one, the Lord wouldn't have called us all, and even if He called all, He wouldn't have promised, 'I will give you to drink.' He could have said, 'Come all of you, for in the end you won't lose anything, and to those whom I choose I will give to drink.' But since He spoke without this condition to all, I hold as certain that all those who do not falter on the way will drink this living water" (*W* 113).

This affirmation is explicit: God calls each one of us personally, individually, and wishes to give us contemplation, on condition that we go on to the end and do not stop on the road halfway.

But doubt may arise in regard to what Teresa has said in the preceding chapters, that is, that not all go by the same road: some souls are contemplative, others are not, and the latter, too, can become saints. But if there are saints who are not contemplatives, then the call to contemplation must not be universal.

Intelligent as the Saint was, she could not have failed to see this apparent contradiction. She said that heaven can be reached by different ways and that one of them lacks the gift of contemplation. "It seems I contradicted in the previous chapter what I had said before. When I was consoling those who were not contemplatives, I said that the Lord had different paths by which to go to Him just as there are many dwelling places" (*W* 114).

"Since His Majesty has understood our weakness, He has

provided after the manner of who He is" (*W* 114). Though inviting all to the greatest heights, He does not use force. He does not make it a condition for eternal salvation to accept His invitation.

Besides, not all the saints in heaven have the same degree of charity; this depends on individuals, for God will be generous with generous souls. Since contemplation is a gift of God, Saint Teresa insisted on our generosity. In fact, she insisted that suffering creates the atmosphere in which contemplation is born. Souls who are not very generous are the ones who will not receive contemplation. And, quite naturally, many are frightened by the invitation to go up to Calvary.

But He does not bar the way to anyone. "He did not say: 'some come by this path, and others by another.' Rather, His mercy was so great He excluded no one from striving to come to this fount of life to drink" (*W* 114). And as proof, the Saint used her years of unfaithfulness, during which she had allowed herself to be shackled with affection for creatures. "How rightly might He have excluded me! Now, since He didn't stop me . . . , surely He excludes no one; rather, He calls us publicly, crying aloud. But since He is so good, He does not force us" (*W* 114); one can also go by a longer road, on which one suffers less.

~

Though God invites all, He does not give all to drink in the same manner, even though they correspond with complete generosity. We have examples in Saint Teresa of Jesus and Saint Thérèse of the Child Jesus: the latter certainly did not go by the way described so minutely by the Saint of Avila

and Saint John of the Cross, but who could say that she was
not a contemplative, an enlightened soul, enlightened by
loving experience? She did not experience the many kinds
of prayer described in the writings of these saints, but she
had so much light from God that she herself confesses that
at twenty-two she was inundated with it, even though she
was living in that aridity which was habitual to her.

"In many ways He gives drink to those who wish to follow Him so that no one will go without consolation or die
of thirst. Rivers stream from this overflowing fount, some
large, others small; and sometimes little pools for children—
for that is enough for them, and moreover it would frighten
them to see a lot of water. These children are the ones who
are at the beginning" (*W* 114). In short, one can drink of
the fountain of living water in many ways, and God gives
to each to drink as is best for his soul. This fountain is actually the operation of the Holy Spirit, contemplative light,
which God infuses into the soul by means of the experience
of love. It will differ because of its intimate relationship to
some definite state of prayer, but what does it matter whether
a person be enlightened in an ecstasy or in the midst of his
daily occupations, provided he thus learns God's will for
him more and more clearly?

> So, Sisters, do not fear that you will die of thirst on this
> road. Never is the lack of consoling water such that it can-
> not be endured. Since this is so, take my advice and do not
> stop on the road but, like the strong, fight even to death in
> the search, for you are not here for any other reason than
> to fight. You must always proceed with this determination
> to die rather than fail to reach the end of the journey. If
> even though you so proceed, the Lord should lead you in
> such a way that you are left with some thirst in this life, in

the life that lasts forever He will give you to drink in great plenty. (*W* 114)

"May it please the Lord that we ourselves do not fail" (*W* 114), Teresa concluded; respond to His invitation by the three virtues she recommended so strongly: detachment from all created things, love for each other, and true humility—and by fidelity to prayer.

III

Resolution and Courage

Saint Teresa detailed the healthy, balanced attitude toward contemplation: desire coupled with resignation, with the general awareness that it is a goal to seek, although it remains a free gift of God. By contemplation we mean the divine intimacy toward which the whole interior life is directed.

At this point Saint Teresa began a lengthy explanation of the development of the life of prayer and used the *Pater noster* as a guide. She started with two concepts: first, the individual must resolve to apply himself diligently to prayer as long as he lives (that is, to go on to the end, cost what it may); second, a correct notion of what mental prayer is and the way by which it prepares one for contemplation.

~

Teresa knew human nature, and she realized that there are persons who linger unnecessarily on the brink of determining to dedicate themselves to prayer. Like a good mother and with psychological insight, she sought to encourage

these hesitating persons by suggesting that they apply themselves gradually but consistently: "I don't say that if a person
doesn't have the determination of which I shall speak here,
he should stop trying; for the Lord will continue perfecting
him. And if that person should do no more than take one
step, the step will contain in itself so much power that he
will not have to fear losing it, nor will he fail to be very well
paid" (*W* 115). Then she introduced a comparison with an
indulgenced chaplet: "If [a person] uses [the beads] once, he
gains the indulgences; if he uses them more often, he gains
more" (*W* 115). One who only applies himself to prayer
from time to time will receive a little light on the day he
does so and feel an urge to do it more often; thus he will
grow in his determination.

Here she was not speaking of her daughters. To them
she would say, "For you this is not enough!" Teresa was
writing here to persons living in the secular society who
desired to live a life of prayer patterned after the absolute
dedication to it characteristic of Carmel. Thus she advised
her followers: when you have the occasion, show persons
whom you see are disposed how they can profit by living in
a spirit of prayer. She meant mental prayer particularly, but
whatever kind of prayer is taught to souls will always be of
great profit to them.

An Objection

"Now returning to those who want to journey on this road
and continue until they reach the end, which is to drink
from this water of life, I say that how they are to begin
is very important—in fact, all important. They must have
a great and very resolute determination to persevere until

reaching the end" (*W* 117), not merely for some periods of life, but for all of it, with all their hearts, to make their prayer ever more intimate, and to drink of this fountain. All do not drink in the same way, yet all should drink. "Come what may, happen what may, whatever work is involved, whatever criticism arises . . ." (*W* 117).

But now Teresa paused to answer an objection common in her time: "There are dangers. . . . The Our Father and the Hail Mary are sufficient" (*W* 118).

When Saint Teresa began to practice prayer in earnest and mentioned this to her spiritual friends, they were frightened and, believing her deluded by the devil, tried to put her on her guard. The Saint began to live in fear, until she met with theologians expert in this doctrine. We ought not be surprised, since great confusion had been caused in Spain at that time by certain deluded persons; thus, when there was question of the graces of prayer, many feared. "You will hear some persons frequently making objections: 'there are dangers'; 'so-and-so went astray by such means'; 'this other one was deceived'; 'another who prayed a great deal fell away'; 'it's harmful to virtue'; 'it's not for women, for they will be susceptible to illusions'; 'it's better they stick to their sewing'; 'they don't need these delicacies'; 'the Our Father and the Hail Mary are sufficient'" (*W* 118).

The Saint had a ready answer: "This last statement, Sisters, I agree with. And indeed they are sufficient!" (*W* 118), but I will show you what the *Pater noster* contains.

> It is always good to base your prayer on prayers coming from the mouth of the Lord. In this matter those who warn us are right, for if our nature were not so weak and our devotion so lukewarm there wouldn't be any need to compose other prayers, nor would there be need for other books. As I say, I am speaking to souls that cannot recollect

their minds in the thought of other mysteries, . . . minds
so ingenious that they're never satisfied with any of their
thoughts. So it seems to me now that I should proceed by
setting down some points here about the beginning, the
means, and the end of prayer. I shall not take time to dwell
on more sublime things. (*W* 118)

This is the plan of the fourth part of her book, for which
she employed the *Pater noster.*

In Spain, the reaction against Protestantism had been vig-
orous; to remove all danger, the Inquisition had forbidden a
quantity of books—among them some dear to Saint Teresa.
She alluded to this fact: "No one will be able to take from
you these books (the Our Father and the Hail Mary), and if
you are eager to learn you won't need anything else provided
you are humble" (*W* 118). And she added a parenthetical
thought that we find also in Saint Thérèse: "I have always
been fond of the words of the Gospels . . . and found more
recollection in them than in very cleverly written books"
(*W* 118).

"I don't say that I'm going to write a commentary on these
divine prayers, for I wouldn't dare. Many commentaries have
been written. . . . But I will mention some thoughts on the
words of the Our Father" (*W* 118) as a point of departure
to teach us to pray, to speak with God.

As a second answer to the objection, Saint Teresa showed
that we are all journeying to this fountain which is God Himself, and we shall all reach it in eternity. This fountain of
living water is the possession of God, but beginning even in
this life, we can drink of it, some in one way, some in another. All are aiming at this fount; well then, by prayer they
travel on a king's highway. On any other way they will die
of thirst: "There are incomparably more dangers for such
persons, but people don't know about them until they bump

blindly into the true danger when there is no one to give them a hand; and they lose the water entirely. . . . How will one journey without a drop of this water on a road where there are so many struggles?" (*W* 119).

"Well, believe me; and don't let anyone deceive you by showing you a road other than that of prayer" (*W* 119).

And a third rebuttal of the objection: it is an alarm invented by the devil to frighten souls. "Never have I seen such a wicked contrivance" (*W* 120); it is contrary to common sense. It is true that there are some who desire to be thought saintly; in Spain at that very time, the deluded Magdalen of the Cross had gained a whole circle of admirers. But if one person has fallen through his own bad dispositions, how many more have been elevated to great perfection by this way!

"And see how blind the world is, for they fail to consider the many thousands who have fallen into heresies and great evils because they didn't practice prayer but engaged in distractions. And if in order to carry on his work better, the devil has caused, among this multitude of persons, some of those who practiced prayer to fall, he has caused as much fear in others about virtuous things. Those who take this reasoning as a refuge in order to free themselves should be on their guard, for they are running away from good in order to free themselves from evil" (*W* 120).

Therefore, we have to react against such deceptions of the devil. "In the midst of these fears the desire not to give up increases within [the real servant of God]. . . . Sometimes one or two men alone can do more when they speak the truth than many together! . . . If they are told there is danger in prayer, one of these servants of God will strive, if not in words then in deeds, to make known how good prayer is. If they are told that frequent Communion is not good, he will receive more frequently. Thus, since there are one or two who fearlessly do what is best, the Lord at once begins to win back gradually the ground that was lost" (*W* 120–21).

Teresa concluded: "Give up these fears; never pay attention in like matters to the opinion of the crowd. . . . Try to preserve a pure conscience, humility, and contempt for all worldly things; believe firmly what Holy Mother Church holds, and you can be sure you will be walking along a good path" (*W* 121).

In the following chapter (22), the Saint showed that vocal prayer cannot be made well if not accompanied by mental prayer: "If they tell you that the prayer should be vocal, ask, for the sake of more precision, if in vocal prayer the mind and heart must be attentive to what you say. If they answer 'yes'—for they cannot answer otherwise—you will see how they admit that you are forced to practice mental prayer and even experience contemplation if God should give it to you by such a means" (*W* 121).

Keeping on with Prayer

Chapter 23 gives the reasons for life-long application to prayer and speaks then of the hope (for Saint Teresa it was a certainty) of arriving at the fountain.

"There are so many reasons why it is extremely important to begin with great determination that I would have to go on at much length if I mentioned them all. Sisters, I want to mention only two or three" (*W* 125):

—delicacy toward Our Lord;
—to keep the devil from tempting us easily;
—certainty of reaching the fountain of living water.

~

First, it would be indelicate to take back a thing we have once given Our Lord; that is, the time we have decided to devote to prayer. Individuals must "give [it] to Him . . . with our thoughts free of other things . . . wholly determined never to take it back from Him, neither because of trials on this account, nor because of contradictions, nor because of dryness. I should consider the time of prayer as not belonging to me and think that He can ask it of me in justice when I do not want to give it wholly to Him" (*W* 126). One who dispenses himself easily from prayer or who, although going to it, does not try to make it well, but yields to distractions, really takes back the time given to Our Lord.

And again we must remember that Teresa wrote for all, people in the world as well as for her daughters; thus she here wished to stimulate the former to prayer as much as she could.

"Another reason for beginning with determination is that the devil will not then have so free a hand to tempt" (*W* 126). The devil, when he sees a person resolved to go on, does not dare to attack, while he readily tempts a timorous, uncertain person. He acts like a dog who does not molest a calm, determined person but chooses instead to torment a timorous person. "He's extremely afraid of determined souls" (*W* 126). There is no need to fear the devil: he is "cowardly. But if the devil should see carelessness, he would do great harm. . . . I know this very well through experience, and that's why I'm able to say, and do say, that no one knows how important determination is" (*W* 127).

The third reason is that, by persevering, one will reach the fountain. When a soul is resolved to remain faithful to prayer, he is more apt to make it well; he is like the soldier who fights with great courage because he knows he has to conquer or else die in his enemies' hands.

In conclusion Saint Teresa reminded her readers to be serenely confident along with their firmness.

> It's also necessary to begin with the assurance that if we don't let ourselves be conquered, we will obtain our goal; this without a doubt, for no matter how small the gain, one will end up being very rich. Don't be afraid that the Lord will leave you to die of thirst, for He calls us to drink from this fount. I have already said this and would like to say it many times, for the devil intimidates persons who don't yet fully know the goodness of the Lord through experience, even though they know it through faith. But it is a great thing to have experienced the friendship and favor He shows toward those who journey on this road and how He takes care of almost all the expenses. (*W* 127)

IV

Various Aspects of Prayer

Saint Teresa insisted on two premises before commenting on the *Pater noster*. The first was a firm resolution to persevere in prayer (chaps. 20, 21, and 23). The second, which we shall now discuss, is the correct notion of mental prayer (chaps. 22, 24, and 25).

There are two ways to show what a thing is. One is to define its character; this method the Saint adopted in chapter 3 of her *Life*, where she defined mental prayer: "For mental prayer in my opinion is nothing else than an intimate sharing between friends; it means taking time frequently to be alone with Him who we know loves us."[1] In another classic text, she said that in prayer "the important thing is not to think much, but to love much"[2]—it should be a colloquy with God. From these quotations we can conclude that prayer is principally affective, although reflection cannot be

[1] Saint Teresa of Jesus, *The Book of Her Life*, chap. 36, nos. 12–13, in vol. 1 of *The Collected Works of St. Teresa of Avila*, trans. Kieran Kavanaugh, O.C.D., and Otilio Rodriguez, O.C.D. (Washington, D.C.: ICS Publications, Institute of Carmelite Studies, 1976), 67.

[2] St. Teresa of Jesus, "The Fourth Dwelling Places", chap. 1, no. 7, in *Interior Castle*, in vol. 2 of *The Collected Works of St. Teresa of Avila*, trans. Kieran Kavanaugh, O.C.D., and Otilio Rodriguez, O.C.D. (Washington, D.C.: ICS Publications, Institute of Carmelite Studies, 1980), 319.

excluded, since knowledge is the guide and spur of love, generating in man the conviction that God loves him.

But, besides definition, there is another method of showing what a thing is, namely, to compare it with things that are similar but not exactly like it. This is what Teresa did in the chapters we are considering. She compared mental prayer with vocal prayer (chap. 22 and part of chap. 24) and with contemplation (chap. 25), showing their differences. Then she finished chapter 25 by summarizing the various elements she had pointed out:

> Now you will understand the difference that lies between perfect contemplation and mental prayer. Mental prayer consists of what was explained: being aware and knowing that we are speaking, with whom we are speaking, and who we ourselves are who dare to speak so much with so great a Lord. To think about this and other similar things, of how little we have served Him and how much we are obliged to serve Him, is mental prayer. Don't think it amounts to some other kind of gibberish, and don't let the name frighten you. To recite the Our Father or the Hail Mary or whatever prayers you wish is vocal prayer. But behold what poor music you produce when you do this without mental prayer. (*W* 131-32)

Mental Prayer

Saint Teresa desired to stress certain arguments against those who are inclined to say that mental prayer is unnecessary and that vocal prayer suffices. She was convinced that vocal prayer, although it is not mental prayer, needs mental prayer joined to it if it is to be made well.

"Realize, daughters, that the nature of mental prayer isn't determined by whether or not the mouth is closed" (*W* 121).

One may speak during mental prayer also, if, during the recital of vocal prayers, his mind is totally occupied with God, with the general intention of praising Him, rather than with the meaning of the words pronounced. "If while speaking I thoroughly understand and know that I am speaking with God and I have greater awareness of this than I do of the words I'm saying, mental and vocal prayer are joined" (*W* 121).

If we had to visit some important personage, we would learn the proper title and form to use in speaking with him. Since prayer is conversation with God, is it not right to take the same care in speaking with Him? Even before vocal prayer, we ought to do this, so that it will not be a simple moving of the lips.

"I shall always have to join mental prayer to vocal prayer —when I remember. . . . Who can say that it is wrong, when we begin to recite the Hours or the rosary, to consider whom we are going to speak with, and who we are, so as to know how to speak with Him? Now I tell you, Sisters, if before you begin your vocal prayer you do the great deal that must be done in order to understand these two points well, you will be spending a good amount of time in mental prayer" (*W* 122–23).

Teresa advised turning one's attention to Christ. She did not intend to exclude the Trinity, but she felt that it would be easier that way to ascend to the divinity. "Oh, our Emperor, supreme Power, supreme Goodness, Wisdom itself, without beginning, without end, without any limit to Your works; they are infinite and incomprehensible, a fathomless sea of marvels, with a beauty containing all beauty, strength itself! Oh, God help me, who might possess here all human eloquence and wisdom together in order to know how to explain clearly . . . a number of the many things we can consider in order to have some knowledge of who this Lord and Good of ours is" (*W* 124).

Teresa placed the divine attributes of Christ at this point in order to attract us to Him. It is true we cannot rise to her heights through a simple meditation; yet these are the same attributes taught us by the catechism and proposed to us as themes for meditation. We may not know them so profoundly, but we ought at least to be conscious that we are before God Who is infinite power, wisdom, and goodness. "Bring yourselves to consider and understand whom you are speaking with, or, as you approach, with whom you are about to speak" (*W* 124).

This is the way to begin: a sincere effort to realize that we are in the presence of a great and good God. If mental prayer consists in becoming aware of Him who is God, it is fitting that we apply ourselves to thinking of Him. To aid us, Teresa stresses His divine beauty and grandeur.

Vocal Prayer

In chapter 24, Saint Teresa expands the notion of mental prayer, this time by teaching how to make vocal prayer well. (Here it is evident that even if Saint Teresa was writing to her daughters, she still had not forgotten the needs of other souls, for she said: "Now, then, let us speak again to those souls I mentioned that cannot recollect or tie their minds down in mental prayer or engage in reflection. . . . Perhaps one of these might come to this house, for as I have also said not everyone walks by the same path" [*W* 128].)

To pray well vocally, we should understand what we recite, especially brief, basic prayers like the Our Father, Hail Mary, and Creed. Not that every time we recite these prayers we must think of the words we say, but we should adopt a suitable attitude of mind, realizing to Whom we turn in these prayers. Or we can have one point upon which to fix our attention; for example, in the *Pater*, the phrase "Thy will be done" appeals to one who wishes to live in abandonment; in the Hail Mary, the words "Mother of God" will be welcome to one who loves to recall that everything comes to us through Our Lady's divine Maternity; during the Creed, we could recall that it is a profession of faith or, like Saint Teresa, rejoice at the words "whose kingdom shall have no end" at Mass.

"I don't want to concern myself with [long prayers]. But I will speak of those prayers we are obliged as Christians to recite (such as, the Our Father and the Hail Mary). . . . For when I say, 'I believe,' it seems to me right that I should know and understand what I believe. And when I say, 'Our Father,' it will be an act of love to understand who this Father of our is and who the Master is who taught us this prayer" (*W* 128–29). Since prayer is a conversation, it is not enough just to understand what we say; we must also be occupied with the one to whom we are speaking.

"It is even a great misfortune if we forget those who teach us here below. Especially, if they are saints and spiritual masters and we are good disciples, it is impossible to forget them [but we love them very much and even take pride in them and often speak of them]. Well, God never allows us to forget the Master who taught us this prayer, and with so much love and desire that it benefit us. He wants us to remember Him often when we say the prayer, even though because of our weakness we do not remember Him always" (*W* 129).

Here Teresa's common sense caused her to foresee days of ill-health and fatigue, when one cannot concentrate. But "whoever experiences the affliction these distractions cause will see that they are not his fault'', and God will see the good will. "He should not grow anxious, which makes things worse, or tire himself trying to put order into . . . his mind. He should just pray as best he can" (*W* 129–30).

"What we ourselves can do is strive to be alone; and please God it will suffice, as I say, that we understand to whom we are speaking and the answer the Lord makes to our petitions" (*W* 130). To pray well, we should place ourselves in favorable circumstances, above all in solitude, not only exterior, but especially interior, in order not to be distracted by any other thought and be able to think of God alone. Jesus recommended, "But when you pray, go into your room and shut the door and pray to your Father who is in secret" (Mt 6:6). This is figurative language used to make us understand that, to speak to our heavenly Father, we ought to be recollected.

"Do you think He is silent?" God does not make His voice heard, but answers by sending grace, light, stimulus to go to Him with more decision. "Even though we do not hear Him, He speaks well to the heart when we beseech Him from the heart" (*W* 130).

"And it is good for us to consider that He taught this prayer to each of us and that He is showing it to us; the teacher is never so far from his pupil that he has to shout, but he is very close. I want you to understand that it is good for you, if you are to recite the Our Father well, to remain at the side of the Master who taught this prayer to you" (*W* 130).

Whoever prays vocally in this way is already making mental prayer: "You will say that doing so involves reflection and that you neither can nor want to pray any other way but vocally" (*W* 130). But how can we make vocal prayer well in any other way? "There are also impatient persons who like to avoid any suffering. Since such individuals do not have the habit, it is difficult for them to recollect their minds in the beginning; and so as to avoid a little fatigue, they say they neither can nor know how to do anything else than pray vocally" (*W* 130).

Yet this effort is necessary to fulfill the "obligation that we strive to pray with attention. . . . Be patient and strive to make a habit out of something that is so necessary" (*W* 130).

Contemplation

With chapter 25, Saint Teresa finished her explanation of the nature of mental prayer; here she compared it with contemplation. First, however, she repeated the necessity of uniting mental prayer with vocal prayer and showed how it can help persons who do experience difficulty in meditating.

"To keep you from thinking that little is gained through a perfect recitation of vocal prayer, I tell you that it is very possible that while you are reciting the Our Father or some other vocal prayer, the Lord may raise you to perfect contemplation" (*W* 131). God speaks to the heart, she had just said, when the heart speaks to Him—and this answer of God is contemplation.

This is a comfort for the many persons who cannot manage to meditate. To put one's whole heart into his vocal prayer is all that is necessary to reach contemplation, if it pleases God to grant it. We have an example in Saint Thérèse. Meditation was not easy for her: she often helped herself with a book or with vocal prayers recited slowly; she did all she could despite the difficulties she experienced, and it was in the midst of these difficulties that God enlightened her. His visits were moments of contemplation, though not a contemplation as sublime as that of which Saint Teresa spoke. She referred to perfect unitive contemplation, which belongs to persons who have reached perfection.

In this state, the individual is absorbed in God, Who gives him a knowledge that is no longer conceptual, but experimental. The divine action, by inflaming the will, enkindles a new light in the intellect and produces a very sublime type of contemplation. Saint John of the Cross, in his *Canticle*, gave the following explanation:

> Since this touch of God gives intense satisfaction and enjoyment to the substance of the soul, and gently fulfills her desire for this union, . . . this most subtle and delicate knowledge penetrates with wonderful savoriness into the innermost part of the substance of the soul, and the delight is greater than all others. The reason for the delight is that the already understood substance, stripped of accidents and phantasms, is bestowed. For this knowledge is given to that intellect which philosophers call the passive or possible intellect, and the intellect receives it passively without any efforts of its own. This knowing is the soul's main delight because it is pertinent to the intellect, and as theologians say fruition, the vision of God, is proper to the intellect.[3]

Saint Teresa discussed unitive contemplation at length throughout her works, especially in chapter 18 of the *Life* and in the Fifth and Sixth Dwelling Places of the *Interior Castle*. But here she merely touched upon it: "The soul understands that without the noise of words this divine Master is teaching it by suspending its faculties, for if they were to be at work they would do harm rather than bring benefit" (*W* 131).

[3] Saint John of the Cross, *The Spiritual Canticle*, stanza 14, no. 14, in *The Collected Works of St. John of the Cross*, trans. Kieran Kavanaugh, O.C.D., and Otilio Rodriguez, O.C.D. (Washington, D.C.: ICS Publications, Institute of Carmelite Studies, 1979), 468.

We must bear in mind that, until God gives contemplation, we should not try to force ourselves into it; instead, we should prepare ourselves by recollection, meditation, and remaining in God's presence with a simple loving attention. When God attracts the soul and causes it enjoyment by quieting all its faculties, then it should receive the gift with simplicity and remain quiet. "[The faculties] are enjoying without understanding how they are enjoying" (*W* 131). At this point, the intellect ceases to reflect and instead rests in God's presence.

Since it is by reasoning that we understand, when the reason does not function, we do not understand; instead, we know by experience. "There is an understanding by not understanding", Teresa wrote, and the expression was so correct that Saint John of the Cross adopted it himself.[4] The person feels that he is united to God but cannot express how because he cannot form ideas.

"The soul is being enkindled in love, and it doesn't understand how it loves. It knows that it enjoys what it loves, but it doesn't know how. It clearly understands that this joy is not a joy the intellect obtains merely through desire. The will is enkindled without understanding how" (*W* 131).

When these moments are over, the intellect recalls what has happened and is convinced that it has tasted God Him-

---

[4] Saint Teresa of Jesus, *Life*, chap. 18, no 14, in *Collected Works*, 121. Saint John of the Cross, "Stanzas concerning an Ecstasy Experienced in High Contemplation", stanza 3, in *Collected Works*, 719. The Saint means that it is an understanding unlike our ordinary and connatural understanding: the latter is "conceptual", i.e., it proceeds with distinct ideas that come from the senses; the former proceeds from another source: the experience of the will, and therefore is not conceptual.

The prayer of union opens wide for the soul the door of a new world that, in the prayer of quiet, was scarcely half-open. Now it will see itself gradually immersed more and more until it loses itself there altogether.

self: "As soon as it can understand something, it sees that this good cannot be merited or gained through all the trials one can suffer on earth. This good is a gift from the Lord of earth and heaven, who, in sum, gives according to who He is. What I have described, daughters, is perfect contemplation" (*W* 131).

Thus, even persons who cannot read can reach contemplation. God in His love takes them and brings them there. And this means perfect (experimental) contemplation, for as we have said, Teresa always meant this when setting contemplation as a goal for her children.

~

At this point, Teresa discussed all three ideas—contemplation, mental prayer, and vocal prayer—together.

Mental prayer "consists of what was explained: being aware and knowing that we are speaking, with whom we are speaking, and who we ourselves are who dare to speak so much with so great a Lord" (*W* 131). For example, in reciting the Our Father, let us see what we can learn by considering just one word, "Father". Who cannot pause here and think: then I *am* His child? And who am I? Nothing but misery by myself, and yet my soul is beautiful by what it has received from Him. He has clothed our poverty in His grace; here is the supernatural reality described so well by Saint John of the Cross in the *Spiritual Canticle*.[5] All the mystery of grace is contained here. And grace is the gift of Him Who is love.

Now we understand by reason alone that God loves His creature. But to gain a really deep knowledge of this truth,

[5] Cf. St. John of the Cross, *Spiritual Canticle*, stanza 37.

we need faith, also. When we know a thing by reasoning, we cling to it only with the intellect; but the whole soul, intellect and will, takes part in knowing by faith and is completely captivated by the truths known. Faith's knowledge belongs to the intellect but is acquired under the impulse of the will.

Thus, for example, as we consider the word "Father", faith will inspire great trust in Him. If we avoid the useless reasonings to which we are so prone—which make the soul unhappy and tense and do not actually give it security—and rest on our faith in God's love for us, we shall advance. Even in the most painful circumstances, we will be certain of being united to God, of becoming transformed into Him by love. The cross is the instrument of detachment and, therefore, of sanctity.

In conclusion, we note with Saint Teresa that "in these two kinds of prayer [vocal and mental], we can do something ourselves, with the help of God" (*W* 132) and ought to do so, but in contemplation "we can do nothing"—all depends on God and to try to procure it for ourselves is ridiculous. Our part is to prepare for it by application to vocal and mental prayer; then, if God "takes the words out of our mouth", we shall be listening.

PART IV

THE LIFE OF PERFECTION

Based on Saint Teresa's
Commentary on the Our Father

I

Meditation

"Our Father"

From chapter 26 to the end of the book, Saint Teresa showed how mental prayer can be practiced so that it gradually becomes contemplative. She based herself on a vocal prayer, the *Pater noster*, and through it showed how to enter into the heart of prayer.

In preparation, to recall the presence of God, she indicated Jesus as the Master teaching us the *Pater*. Then she traveled the whole road of prayer from beginning to end by considering the petitions one by one.

In the Presence of God

The first thing is to recall God's presence, and this may be done in various ways. The Saint gave one—for the person who cannot meditate by reflecting on the points in a book and has to use a vocal prayer instead. But from this one way, we can draw the general principles and apply them to all the other ways.

"As is already known, the examination of conscience, the act of contrition, and the sign of the cross must come first"

(*W* 133). She was alluding to the practice then in use in all monasteries, and it is one way of beginning. Nowadays we usually begin prayer with the "Come, Holy Spirit . . .", which fills the same purpose by requesting help.

"Then, daughters, since you are alone, strive to find a companion. Well what better companion than the Master Himself who taught you this prayer? Represent the Lord Himself as close to you and behold how lovingly and humbly He is teaching you" (*W* 133). Even if we spent the whole time of prayer just gazing on the adorable Person of Our Lord, we would make excellent prayer.

"Believe me, you should remain with so good a friend as long as you can. If you grow accustomed to having Him present at your side, and He sees that you do so with love and that you go about striving to please Him, you will not be able—as they say—to get away from Him; He will never fail you; He will help you in all your trials; you will find Him everywhere. Do you think it's some small matter to have a friend like this at your side?" (*W* 133). Saint Teresa was referring to that presence which we ought to cultivate, not only during prayer, but also during the day. If we form this habit, we shall find it easy to intensify its acts on beginning prayer.

"O Sisters, those of you who cannot engage in much discursive reflection with the intellect or keep your mind from distraction, get used to this practice! Get used to it! See, I know that you can do this" (*W* 133). The Saint delighted in saying that on the way to union with God there are many things we can do ourselves.

Saint Thérèse, speaking of her conversion on Christmas night, said that in a moment God worked in her what she had not succeeded in doing in many years, despite all the efforts of her constant good will.

"I suffered many years from the trial—and it is a very great one—of not being able to quiet the mind in anything. But I know that the Lord does not leave us so abandoned; for if we humbly ask Him for this friendship, He will not deny it to us. And if we cannot succeed in one year, we will succeed later. Let's not regret the time that is so well spent. Who's making us hurry? I am speaking of acquiring this habit and of striving to walk alongside this true Master" (*W* 133).

Teresa's reason for establishing direct contact with God from the very beginning of prayer followed from her notion of prayer: a friendly conversation. To speak intimately with a person, one has to have him near. Many souls waste time in prayer because they are careless about this initial contact. Distractions may come afterward, but one will get back to recollection more easily because of this beginning.

If we call upon God, it is to occupy ourselves with Him, so we need to look at Him; we are free to use any mystery we like. Here the Saint has some beautiful pages that reveal her own method a little. "If you are joyful, look at Him as risen. Just imagining how He rose from the tomb will bring you joy. The brilliance! The beauty! The majesty! How victorious! How joyful!" (*W* 134).

> If you are experiencing trials or are sad, behold Him on the way to the garden: what great affliction He bore in His soul; for having become suffering itself, He tells us about it and complains of it. Or behold Him bound to the column, filled with pain, with all His flesh torn in pieces for the great love He bears you; so much suffering. . . . Or behold Him burdened with the cross, for they didn't even let Him take a breath. He will look at you with those eyes so beautiful and compassionate, filled with tears; He will forget His sorrows so as to console you in yours, merely

because you yourselves go to Him to be consoled, and you
turn your head to look at Him. (*W* 134–35)

There is no question of reflection as in meditation. It suffices to think of Jesus in some mystery, looking at Him:
"O Lord of the world, my true Spouse! (You can say this
to Him if He has moved your heart to pity at seeing Him
thus, for not only will you desire to look at Him but you
will also delight in speaking with Him, not with ready-made
prayers but with those that come from the sorrow of your
own heart, for He esteems them highly.) Are You so in need,
my Lord and my Love, that You would want to receive such
poor company as mine, for I see by Your expression that
You have been consoled by me?" (*W* 135). This contact
with God is the essence of prayer, and we can reach it right
from the beginning.

Of course, effort is necessary: "You will ask, Sisters, how
you can do this, saying that if you had seen His Majesty with
your bodily eyes at the time He walked in this world that
you would have looked at Him very willingly and done so
always. Don't believe it. Whoever doesn't want to use a little
effort now to recollect at least the sense of sight and look at
this Lord within herself (for one can do so without danger
but with just a little care) would have been much less able
to stay at the foot of the cross with the Magdalene, who
saw His death with her own eyes" (*W* 135–36).

This doctrine can be applied to other ways of recalling the
presence of God, for we are free to use any we may wish:
thinking of Jesus in the Eucharist, of the Blessed Trinity,
or of one of the Divine Persons. Or we can recall that God
is present in us—in His immensity, His power, and His
essence: He is our Creator. Again we can remember our
dependence on Him—Teresa herself loved to do this. Or

we can remind ourselves that the Blessed Trinity is dwelling in us in order to be known, loved, and in a certain manner enjoyed, even beginning during this life. It is worth a little effort to realize this divine presence, whatever be the degree of prayer we have reached!

For those moments when circumstances cause us to come to prayer somewhat distracted, Teresa suggested ways of returning gently to the presence of God: "What you can do as a help in this matter is try to carry about an image or painting of this Lord that is to your liking, not so as to carry it about on your heart and never look at it but so as to speak often with Him; for He will inspire you with what to say" (*W* 136). As a good illustration of this, we need only recall how Saint Thérèse used the image of the Holy Face to overcome her many difficulties in prayer. "It is also a great help to take a good book written in the vernacular" (*W* 136) that speaks of God.

One who begins prayer dynamically, by coming into God's presence, will readily learn what intimate contact with Him is. "If with care you grow accustomed to what I have said, your gain will be so great that even if I wanted to explain this to you I wouldn't know how" (*W* 137).

First Degree of Prayer

In chapter 27 Teresa wrote about the first degree of prayer, which is meditation. She did so, keeping before her the image of one who cannot follow the "classical manner" of meditating.

Let us suppose that this person has prepared himself by recalling God's presence. Since he cannot delve into a mystery and draw out practical lessons as he finds it in a meditation book, he begins his vocal prayer by saying: *Our Father who art in heaven*. Since the Saint expected mental prayer to be united to vocal, these first words of the *Pater noster* give him occasion for an affectionate conversation with God. There are only two parts to this meditation suggested by the Saint:

1. the loving colloquy, fired by the thought of God's love for us and a desire to love Him in return;

2. practical application to our life.

Loving Conversation with God

The words *Our Father Who art in heaven* made Teresa exclaim: "O my Lord, how You do show Yourself to be the Father of such a Son; and how Your Son does show Himself to be the Son of such a Father! May You be blessed forever and ever! This favor would not be so great, Lord, if it came at the end of the prayer. But at the beginning, You fill our hands and give a reward so large that it would easily fill the intellect and thus occupy the will in such a way one would be unable to speak a word" (*W* 137). She was trying her best to make us realize God's love and to pray with childlike trust, considering Him, not as Creator and supreme Ruler, but as our Father who loves and cares for us.

So great a truth would be enough to captivate a soul and place it in contemplation. "Oh, daughters, how readily should perfect contemplation come at this point! Oh, how right it would be for the soul to enter within itself in order to rise the better above itself that this holy Son might make it understand the nature of the place where He says His Father dwells, which is in the heavens" (*W* 137). However, the Saint did not yet speak of contemplation because she first had to explain the lower grades of prayer wherein the soul has to work for itself.

She began to converse with Jesus, Who makes us say, like Himself, *Our Father*. Like Him, we are sons of God: He by nature, we by adoption; but we do belong to the divine Family.

> O Son of God and my Lord! How is it that You give so much all together in the first words? Since You humble Yourself to such an extreme in joining with us in prayer and making Yourself the Brother of creatures so lowly and wretched, how is it that You give us in the name of Your Father everything that can be given? For You desire that He consider us His children, because Your word cannot fail. You oblige Him to be true to Your word, which is no small burden since in being Father He must bear with us no matter how serious the offenses. If we return to Him like the prodigal son, He has to pardon us. He has to console us in our trials. He has to sustain us in the way a father like this must. For, in effect, He must be better than all the fathers in the world because in Him everything must be faultless. And after all this He must make us sharers and heirs with You. (*W* 138)

As one can meditate on the Passion—for example, Jesus at the column—to move oneself to love Him, so here the recital of the *Our Father* serves as spur to reflection. It is simply a different approach at a better grasp of God's great love for us with a consequent deepening of our love for Him.

"Behold, my Lord, that since with the love You bear us and with Your humility, nothing will stop you . . . in sum, Lord, You are on earth and clothed with it. Since You possess our nature, it seems You have some reason to look to our gain. But behold, Your Father is in heaven. You

Yourself said so. It is right that You look to His honor. . . .
O good Jesus! How clearly You have shown that You are
one with Him, and that Your will is His and His, Yours!
. . . How magnificent it is, the love You bear us!" (*W* 138).

Resolutions

Every good meditation should have a practical side, also.
Therefore, in the second part of this chapter, the Saint suggested some resolutions for those just entering upon a life
of prayer.

"Does it seem right to you now that even though we
recite these first words vocally we should fail to let our in-
tellects understand and our hearts break in pieces at seeing
such love?" (*W* 139). And so the first resolution: to seek
to know God's lovableness better and better. "What son is
there in the world who doesn't strive to learn who his father
is when he knows he has such a good one with so much
majesty and power?" (*W* 139).

The second resolution is more general: "You have a good
Father, for He gives you the good Jesus. Let no one in this
house speak of any other father but Him. And strive, my
daughters, so to behave that you will deserve to find your
delight in Him; and cast yourselves into His arms" (*W* 139).
This is simply to recall the ideal of intimacy with God, *together with* the life of generosity that should prepare one for
reaching it. "You already know that He will not reject you
if you are good daughters. Who, then, would fail to strive
so as not to lose such a Father?" (*W* 139–40).

Thus we have a real meditation, a meditation that is within
everyone's power. Who can say he is unable to recite the
Our Father and think of the meaning of the words? And

how can one aware of this great love fail to make generous resolutions? Recollection during the day will come more easily, because a genuine loving conversation with God in prayer can only intensify one's awareness of God's presence.

Saint Teresa ended this section with a reflection on the Trinity that is interesting because she had not yet had that Trinitarian experience which she would enjoy ten years later: "However much your thoughts may wander, between such a Son and such a Father the Holy Spirit must perforce be found. May He enkindle your will and bind you to Himself with the most fervent love, since even your own great gain suffices not to urge you to it."

II

The Prayer of Recollection

"Who art in heaven"

With chapter 28 Teresa began speaking of another form of prayer that, in a wide sense, can be called a second step, because in it recollection is more intense than in ordinary prayer and yet it does begin a new phase in the growth of prayer.[1]

Second Degree of Prayer

Although Saint Teresa described it, we can comprehend the prayer of recollection easier by saying that it is, quite simply, the realization of the presence of God in us. This means an *active* realization (not the passive one that belongs to infused prayer of which Saint Teresa wrote at length in chapter 3 of the Fourth Dwelling Places of the *Interior Castle*), an active realization obtained as the result of the combined effort of the mind and will enlightened by faith. Thus it does have something in common with the preceding degree, which

---

[1] Teresa spoke of the prayer of recollection in chapters 28 and 29: first, of its nature and advantages; then, of the way to obtain it. The first three paragraphs of chap. 29 are a digression on an exercise of humility.

—as we have seen—begins with an act of the presence of God; but here there is a realization of God within us. This is to become the major occupation of the soul. Later, one can apply himself to other forms of prayer, whether vocal or meditative.

However, since the senses, the imagination, and the intellect are like many windows open on the external world through which we easily go out and get lost, a person who wishes to remain in God's company within himself must apply these powers to an interior object: God. He, as an object of knowledge, is always within us although we are unaware of it. He can make Himself felt, but that depends upon Him.

How can we relate ourselves to this interior object? The answer: through the gaze of faith.

I do not say that a philosopher, learned in metaphysics, cannot make himself conscious of the presence of God within us, but few have his capacity to grasp by reason alone that, since the Creator is immense and all-powerful, He is in all creatures. And so God *revealed* His presence of immensity (as it is called); consequently, all can know it by faith.

Faith speaks of another presence of God in the soul that reason alone could not discover: the presence of the Blessed Trinity through grace. Unlike the presence of immensity, this is not simply a presence of activity—the activity of preserving us in existence; it is rather a presence of *living together*, wherein God shares His life with us. Through sanctifying grace, God comes to dwell in the soul as in His temple, and it can place itself in vital contact with Him by knowledge and love. God offers Himself to us to be known, loved, and enjoyed, even on earth.

However, man's enjoyment of God is passive—he cannot procure it by himself—because it stems from the gifts of the Holy Spirit. Yet every man in the state of grace possesses these gifts and, consequently, possesses also the immediate possibility of enjoying God.

One may say, then, that God offers Himself to man to be enjoyed when *He* wills, but to be known and loved when *we* will, because the theological virtues suffice for this. For a loving, filial contact, faith suffices. Faith is true but obscure knowledge, wrote Saint John of the Cross.

The essence of the prayer of recollection is an intense exercise of the theological virtues.

Man's soul is a little heaven in which he can enclose himself to live with God. Retiring from creatures, he seeks the Trinity, and his "eye of faith" finds It. And after he has been faithful to this for a while, Teresa insisted, he finds that he can converse familiarly with God, that he can look at Him and speak to Him, not necessarily in words—though these will often come. Man's wordless love is enough, and God will answer with His lights. True, he does not perceive the divine action; but it is nonetheless real. There is no new interior experience, but God is at the gates.

Consequently, man should calm his faculties, withdraw his senses from external things, and concentrate on God present in him.

"Anyone who walks by this path keeps his eyes closed almost as often as he prays. This is a praiseworthy custom for many reasons. It is a striving so as not to look at things here below. This striving comes at the beginning; afterward, there's no need to strive; a greater effort is needed to open the eyes while praying" (*W* 142). Even the imagination keeps quiet, so that the intellect can apply itself more easily to God, and the recollection is thus intensified. This form of prayer habituates us little by little to remain in God's company.

Once we have realized God's presence in us, a life of union with Him begins, because this is not just an *act* for beginning prayer, as it was in the preceding stage; it is the substance of this prayer. It becomes easier to sustain a vital awareness throughout the day, and not just at prayer time.

And at prayer itself, after renewing this intimate contact with God, one can continue his prayer in any form: either prolonging the look of simple love, reciting vocal prayers in the way Saint Teresa has taught, continuing his loving colloquy, or making a true and proper meditation—for example, on the Passion—with Jesus Who is there, in his inmost soul.

The prayer of recollection can be combined with any form of prayer.

Advantages

Teresa noted that there are many grades of recollection: it can be more or less intense, according to one's efforts. Not that its intensity depends entirely on us—for our psychological condition does affect it—but its advantages depend upon its intensity.

The Saint indicated three of these benefits:

1. *Man acquires a certain dominion over his senses.* His effort to calm them and keep them from following their impressions makes him, to some degree, master of them. Now he can pacify them, not only in general, during the day, but especially during the time of prayer. It is important not to allow oneself to be distracted by what occurs about him, Saint John of the Cross recommends.[2] There will always be

---

[2] Cf. St. John of the Cross, third *Precaution* "Against the World": "Very

some activity in the intellect, he said,[3] and from time to time the imagination will distract it, but if one has begun well, it becomes easier to return to recollection.

2. *The love of God is inflamed more easily* in a man who is recollected because he is more vividly aware of God's presence.

3. *The prayer of recollection disposes man for infused prayer.* His transit to infused prayer may happen without his conscious awareness of it. A man who is actively recollected attracts God to himself, and thus the prayer of recollection provides the best preparation for the prayer of quiet. Saint Teresa often mentioned this preparation for infused prayer and even spoke of its relationship to perfect contemplation: "After many of these entries [the senses returning to the soul, after having been recalled by the will to recollection] the Lord wills that they rest entirely in perfect contemplation" (*W* 143).

---

carefully guard yourself against thinking about what happens in the community, and even more against speaking of it. . . . Should you desire to pay heed to things, many will seem wrong, even though you may live among angels, because of your not understanding the nature of them. . . .

"God's will [is that you] . . . strive to keep your soul occupied purely and entirely in God, and not let the thought of this thing or that hinder you from so doing. . . . If you do not guard yourself . . . you will be unable to . . . attain holy denudation and recollection." In *The Collected Works of St. John of the Cross*, trans. Kieran Kavanaugh, O.C.D., and Otilio Rodriguez, O.C.D. (Washington, D.C.: ICS Publications, Institute of Carmelite Studies, 1979), 657–58.

[3] St. John of the Cross, *The Ascent of Mount Carmel*, bk. 2, chap. 12, no. 8: "The advice proper for these individuals is that they must learn to abide in that quietude with a loving attentiveness to God and pay no heed to the imagination and its work." In *Collected Works*, 139.

Chap. 13, no. 3: "I am not affirming that the imagination will cease to come and go (even in deep recollection it usually wanders freely), but that the person is disinclined to fix it purposely upon extraneous things." In *Collected Works*, 140.

Helpful Practices

Saint Teresa suggested three practices that can help us acquire this prayer of active recollection. The first two pertain to the beginning of prayer, and the third is for the remainder of the day to facilitate recollection.

Prayer consists in acts of knowledge and love. Although love effects union, it must be guided by knowledge: before I can love God, I have to know that He exists. So the first of these three practices is for the intellect: a practical way of realizing God's presence in us. In another manner of speaking, we can say that it is a realization of our interior wealth, for Saint Teresa spoke of this divine presence in relation to the grace and virtues we possess and which should be cultivated in order to increase union with God.

> Well, let us imagine that within us is an extremely rich palace, built entirely of gold and precious stones; in sum, built for a lord such as this. Imagine, too, as is indeed so, that you have a part to play in order for the palace to be so beautiful; for there is no edifice as beautiful as is a soul pure and full of virtues. The greater the virtues the more resplendent the jewels. Imagine, also, that in this palace dwells this mighty King who has been gracious enough to become your Father; and that He is seated upon an extremely valuable throne, which is your heart. (*W* 143–44)

"Let's not imagine that we are hollow inside" (*W* 144); we have within us riches that she deplored not having known for many years, due to ignorance. "And please God", she added, "it may be only women that go about forgetful of this inner richness and beauty" (*W* 144). Here she evidently alluded to an incident recounted in her *Life*: she asked a certain theologian about this presence of God in us, and he was unable to answer her.

She spoke of the presence of God in us along with the retinue of virtues that accompany grace. The palace can always be made more magnificent because we can develop this wealth deposited in the soul by baptism. In a certain sense, we can say that the Blessed Trinity grows ever nearer to us, because, as virtue increases in the soul, we are ever more prepared to enter into dynamic contact with God.

But this first practice, aimed at the intellect, is inadequate to attain intimate union with God.

At this point, we find that famous maxim: "Since [Christ] doesn't force our will, He takes what we give Him; but He doesn't give Himself completely until we give ourselves completely" (*W* 145). This expresses the essence of Teresian spirituality: man must open his whole soul and let it be invaded by the divine will.

Expressive of this is Saint Thérèse's act of oblation: "O my God . . . I offer myself as a victim of holocaust to Your merciful love", to Your will; that is, to be always pleased with what You do and at the same time to try always to please You. Her abandon is anything but passivity; it is active adherence to God's will. A good way to pray when one has difficulty in meditating is to recite this act of oblation to merciful Love slowly.

God "never works in the soul as He does when it is totally His without any obstacle, nor do I see how He could. He is the friend of all good order" (*W* 145).

When God unites man to Himself, He expands him so that he can enter spiritually into an immense depth, but this depends upon his giving God his whole will. He seeks man's permission; man has to open the gate so that God can enter and attract the soul to Himself.

If God is in the soul as in a heaven, said the Saint, returning to those words of the *Pater noster* upon which she was commenting ("Who art in heaven"), the saints who form His court will also be with Him in some manner.

Actually, they are present only insofar as they know and see in God what we do in their honor. Teresa noted that their presence does not impede our solitude with Him, nor will it do so in heaven. Man will always be a great solitary, insofar as the substantial beatitude of the solitary life is concerned. The secrets uttered to the soul in the beatific vision are incommunicable.

The two great instruments by which man procures the prayer of recollection, therefore, are his realization of his inner wealth by awareness of God's presence and then his gift of his whole self to God.

The third practice that prepares man for the prayer of recollection is his practice of the presence of God throughout the day. Many methods of doing this are possible, for example, the use of an external object, a mental recalling of God's presence of immensity or that of indwelling.[4]

> I conclude by saying that whoever wishes to acquire it—since, as I say, it lies within our power—should not tire of getting used to what has been explained. It involves a gradual increase of self-control and an end to vain wandering from the right path; it means conquering, which is a making use of one's senses for the sake of the inner life. If you speak, strive to remember that the One with whom you are speaking is present within. If you listen, remember that you are going to hear One who is very close to you when He speaks. In sum, bear in mind that you can, if you want, avoid ever withdrawing from such good company; and be sorry that for a long time you left your Father alone, of whom you are so much in need. If you can, prac-

[4] Cf. Fr. Gabriel of St. Mary Magdalen, *Little Catechism of Prayer* (Concord, N.H.: Monastery of Discalced Carmelites, 1949), chap. 6.

tice this recollection often during the day; if not, do so a few times. As you become accustomed to it you will experience the benefit, either sooner or later. Once this recollection is given by the Lord, you will not exchange it for any treasure.

Since nothing is learned without a little effort, consider, Sisters, for the love of God, as well employed the attention you give to this method of prayer. I know, if you try, that within a year, or perhaps half a year, you will acquire it, by the favor of God. See how little time it takes for a gain as great as is that of laying a good foundation. If then the Lord should desire to raise you to higher things He will discover in you the readiness, finding that you are close to Him. May it please His Majesty that we not consent to withdrawing from His presence. (*W* 148–49)

III

The Prayer of Quiet

"Hallowed be Thy name;
Thy kingdom come"

Teresa dedicated the next two chapters to the prayer of quiet, a supernatural prayer, which one cannot procure for himself. God Himself, she noted, united the two petitions: *Hallowed be Thy name* and *Thy kingdom come*. "Since His Majesty saw that we could neither hallow, nor praise, nor extol, nor glorify this holy name of the Eternal Father in a fitting way, because of the tiny amount we ourselves are capable of doing, He provided for us by giving us here on earth His kingdom [the prayer of quiet]" (*W* 150), for one cannot praise God perfectly unless one loves Him greatly.

Third Degree of Prayer

This is the second time the Saint raises our thoughts to heaven; the first time she was commenting on the words *Who art in heaven*; now her purpose is to show that, in the prayer of quiet, we foretaste something of what we shall have in Paradise. Her thought rose easily to commerce among the

Blessed; when it returned to this mortal life, it yearned to have all men live in praise of God.

Let us recall the pages of the *Interior Castle* of Saint Teresa[1] and those of the *Spiritual Canticle* of Saint John of the Cross[2] that, explaining fruitive prayer, speak of a sense of exaltation stemming from one's experience of God's goodness. At this point, however, we are not yet speaking of such a lofty development of prayer. Yet when one has tasted God's love, one knows Him better and praises Him more. The heart enamored of God spontaneously renders Him honor and glory, because it knows His lovableness and has experienced His sweetness.

[1] St. Teresa of Jesus, "Sixth Dwelling Places", chap. 6, nos. 10–11, in *Interior Castle*, in vol. 2 of *The Collected Works of St. Teresa of Avila*, trans. Kieran Kavanaugh, O.C.D., and Otilio Rodriguez, O.C.D. (Washington, D.C.: ICS Publications, Institute of Carmelite Studies, 1980), 395–96: "It is, in my opinion, a deep union of the faculties; but our Lord nonetheless leaves them free that they might enjoy this joy—and the same goes for the senses—without understanding what it is they are enjoying or how they are enjoying. . . . The joy is so excessive the soul wouldn't want to enjoy it alone but wants to tell everyone about it so that they might help this soul praise our Lord. . . . St. Francis must have felt this impulse when the robbers struck him, for he ran through the fields crying out and telling the robbers that he was the herald of the great King."

[2] Cf. St. John of the Cross, *The Spiritual Canticle*, stanzas 9, 14, 15. "The soul sees and tastes abundance and inestimable riches in this divine union. She finds all the rest and recreation she desires, and understands secrets and strange knowledge of God, which is another one of the foods that taste best to her. She experiences in God an awesome power and strength which sweeps away every other power and strength. She tastes there a splendid spiritual sweetness and gratification, discovers true quiet and divine light, and tastes sublimely the wisdom of God reflected in the harmony of His creatures and works. She has the feeling of being filled with blessings and of being empty of evils and far removed from them. And above all she understands and enjoys inestimable refreshment of love which confirms her in love" (stanza 14, no. 4), in *The Collected Works of St. John of the Cross*, trans. Kieran Kavanaugh, O.C.D., and Otilio Rodriguez, O.C.D. (Washington, D.C.: ICS Publications, Institute of Carmelite Studies, 1979), 463–64.

Now, then, the great good that it seems to me there will be in the kingdom of heaven, among many other blessings, is that one will no longer take any account of earthly things, but have a calmness and glory within, rejoice in the fact that all are rejoicing, experience perpetual peace and a wonderful inner satisfaction that comes from seeing that everyone hallows and praises the Lord and blesses His name and that no one offends Him. Everyone loves Him there, and the soul itself doesn't think about anything else than loving Him; nor can it cease loving Him, because it knows Him. (*W* 151)

The more deeply one knows Him, with a knowledge that has some of the experimental in it, the more one will be drawn to praise and love Him perfectly, for contemplative knowledge has a certain affinity to the knowledge of the Blessed.

"And would that we could love Him in this way here below, even though we may not be able to do so with such perfection or stability. But if we knew Him we would love in a way very different from that in which we do love Him" (*W* 151).

Naturally we cannot possess the kingdom of heaven yet, for that does not belong to this life; but the Saint observed that, beginning in this life, we can attain it to some degree, and it is this growing possession which the soul acquires by means of prayer and contemplation.

"It seems I'm saying that we would have to be angels in order to make this petition and recite well our vocal prayers" (*W* 151). In a certain sense, this is a true desire—at least insofar as man can imitate their complete absorption in the divine praise. We seek His kingdom, not only in heaven, but also on earth.

So Saint Teresa thought it legitimate to desire this more

profound form of prayer which bestows an experimental knowledge of God.

> Certainly He doesn't tell us to ask for impossible things. The above would be possible, through the favor of God, for a soul placed in this exile, but not with the perfection of those who have gone forth from this prison: for we are at sea and journeying along this way. But there are times when, tired from our travels, we experience that the Lord calms our faculties and quiets the soul. As though by signs, He gives us a clear foretaste of what will be given to those He brings to His kingdom. And to those to whom He gives here below the kingdom we ask for, He gives pledges so that through these they may have great hope of going to enjoy perpetually what here on earth is given only in sips. (*W* 151)

Teresa's thought is this: Christ has united these two petitions *hallowed be Thy name* and *Thy kingdom come* to show us that we should unite them, too. He wishes that we spend our whole life in praise, sustained best by some experimental knowledge of God. Thus begins a very pure degree of contemplation, wherein a man does not employ images and ideas, but proceeds by means of love with a *taste* of God.

The Saint half excused herself for speaking of it when she promised to confine herself to teaching how to make vocal prayer well. But as she did say that often God raises a soul to perfect contemplation from vocal prayer made well, so she availed herself of the opportunity to speak of it, although vocal prayer is actually her subject here. Both go together well, she said. She cited the example of a person she knew who could do nothing save recite the *Pater*, yet she did it with such devotion that she spent whole hours on it and, "though keeping to the *Our Father*, she was experiencing pure contemplation, and occasionally God raised her to perfect union with Himself."

Description of the Prayer of Quiet

At this point (chap. 31), Saint Teresa wrote of her own personal experience. This state of prayer can be realized in various degrees; in this as in other matters, there are no two individuals alike. But this did *not* dismay the Saint, for she seems very comfortable with the idea throughout this book treating of the way of perfection.

She had already described it in her *Life* when she explained the "second manner of drawing water", and she would treat of it again when she wrote the *Interior Castle*.

Using the confidences of her spiritual daughters, Saint Teresa spoke of the varieties of these graces in the light of their experiences, but most of the time she spoke of her own personal experience. "Well, daughters, I nonetheless want to explain this prayer of quiet. I have heard talk about it, or the Lord has given me understanding of it, perhaps, that I might tell you of it" (*W* 153).

"In this prayer it seems the Lord begins, as I have said, to show that He hears our petition. He begins now to give us His kingdom here below so that we may truly praise and hallow His name and strive that all persons do so. This prayer is something supernatural" (*W* 153). What did Saint Teresa mean by supernatural? Even our customary prayers are supernatural, inasmuch as they are raised to the superior order of the grace that we possess. It is not in this sense that the Saint used the word, but in a special sense, for in her thought the initiative comes from God, not from us: it is a *passive* prayer. And here again we must be careful about the meaning of the word. *Passive* does not mean *laissez faire*, with no personal activity, but that we cannot procure this prayer; *we* can only dispose ourselves for it: "something we cannot procure through our own efforts" (*W* 153).

Behind this lies the theological fact that such prayer depends upon the action of the gifts of the Holy Spirit, which do not function because of our efforts; they depend completely upon God. We can only prepare ourselves.

The prayer of quiet is the first contemplative prayer in which man perceives that it is not he alone who is working. Often God has already worked and oriented him without his perceiving it. But suddenly he becomes aware of an orientation of his life that he has not procured by himself but that stems from a deeper spiritual experience.

"In it the soul enters into peace or, better, the Lord puts it at peace by His presence, as He did to the just Simeon, so that all the faculties are calmed. The soul understands in another way, very foreign to the way it understands through the exterior senses, that it is now close to its God and that not much more would be required for it to become one with Him in union" (*W* 153). Union is really a very great intensification of the prayer of quiet.

However, even if the prayer of quiet can be explained by the intervention of the gifts of the Holy Spirit, this intervention does not sufficiently explain the prayer of fruitive union, which requires God's direct action on the will; this theologians call a "divine substantial touch".

"This is not because it sees Him with the eyes either of the body or of the soul" (*W* 153), Saint Teresa continued. The spiritual eyes are the imagination; the bodily, the senses, which put us into contact with exterior objects.

"The just Simeon didn't see any more than the glorious, little, poor child. For the way the child was clothed and by the few people that were in the procession, Simeon could have easily judged the babe to be the son of poor people rather than the Son of our heavenly Father. But the child Himself made Simeon understand. And this is how the soul understands here, although not with as much clarity" (*W* 153), that is, by a knowledge that comes, not through the senses, but from within, from that which the soul experiences. It is a knowledge through love.

Knowledge always comes from some experience, but experience is twofold:

1. from outside, through the senses, as, for example, the sight of a magnificent panorama that makes one say: "How beautiful must the One Who created it be!" And this thought arouses love.

One can also do this with the imagination. Picturing to ourselves a landscape seen at another time, we can form ideas that then inspire us with love of God.

2. interior experience. This is quite another thing.

The love of charity is a friendship, a mutual well-wishing. We desire good things for God, but He desires them much more for us and draws us to Himself. This attraction varies in intensity; at times it is so hidden that a man is unaware of it; at other times, it is so strong that he feels himself the prisoner of God. This transcends the experience of the senses and of the imagination; it is the experience of love; yet it reflects upon the intelligence, not by arousing ideas, but by producing a "sense of God". Man becomes aware that this God by Whom he feels himself taken captive is so unique, so great, so superior to all things that there is nothing comparable to Him. Here it is not a question of ideas awakening love, as in (1) above; on the contrary, the intellect receives knowledge from love.

Without some "sense of God", man cannot properly orient himself to God. By this we do not mean that God is obliged to give this by means of the prayer of quiet. Spiritual experiences were much more discernible in Saint John of the Cross and Saint Teresa of Avila than in Saint Thérèse of Lisieux. For the latter, her "sense of God" was very hidden, though very profound.

The soul "fails to understand how it understands. But it sees it is in the kingdom, at least near the King who will give the kingdom to the soul. And seemingly the soul has so much reverence that it doesn't even dare ask for this" (*W* 153). There is no need for the individual to understand how this happens. The essential thing is not to understand, but to have this experimental knowledge of love.

Where is this attraction coming from God felt?

In the will; therefore, Teresa said, the will feels itself a prisoner. The other faculties, too, can be captivated, but often intellect and memory are free and actually weary the soul with their restless movements.

The will is so contented to be drawn by God into His embrace that it does not want to have its freedom anymore. The Saint always insisted on this in speaking of the prayer of quiet. We recall Saint Augustine: "You have made us for Yourself, O God, and our heart is restless until it rests in You."[3] Here man experiences a peace that diffuses itself throughout his entire being, although there may be obstacles to it from the other two powers that remain free.

Since it is held by God, the will cannot be distracted from

[3] *Confessions*, bk. 1, chap. 1.

Him, while the intellect *can* be, and if the soul follows it, it will be distracted, too, and will disturb the repose of the will. While the will enjoys God, the intellect notices this and seeks to intervene with its own natural work, forming ideas about what the will is enjoying, because its natural tendency is to understand; and the memory contributes its share. However, the intellect finds that it cannot adequately grasp this experience, for it defies expression. Should a man permit himself to follow this natural movement of the intellect and memory and try to form ideas, he will quickly distract himself from the loving attention that occupies the will.

But when God draws the soul still more strongly, the effect on the intellect is so intense that it, too, is quieted. The stronger the attraction in the will, the greater is the "sense of God" in the intellect.

Advice

The first piece of advice Saint Teresa gave was aimed at preventing great indiscretion. There are some who, perceiving these experiences of love, fear to move or even to breathe in order to prolong this sweetness. Teresa reminded them that this is a supernatural thing, which can be neither procured nor prolonged by human industry.

However, it is well at this time to stay in greater solitude and recollection. Saint John of the Cross[4] stated that it is a crime to occupy souls attracted by solitary love in worldly

---

[4] Saint John of the Cross, *Spiritual Canticle*, commentary for stanza 29: "It should be noted that until the soul reaches this state of union of love, she should practice love in both the active and contemplative life. Yet once she arrives, she should not become involved in other works and exterior exercises that might be of the slightest hindrance to the attentiveness of love toward

affairs because solitude is *the* atmosphere for developing these graces and opening the soul to a purer and deeper love. They must try to lead a very recollected life.

Second, Teresa wrote, if in this prayer, one becomes aware that the intellect is trying to grasp what is happening, he must pay no attention to the desire. If he does follow the movement of the mind and try to understand, he will become distracted.

There is only one thing a person can do, and that is to remain quiet; actually, theologians speak of semi-passive prayer. In the prayer of union, the soul will be completely taken over by God and will have nothing more to do.

"A soul to whom God gives such pledges has a sign that He wants to give it a great deal; if not impeded through its own fault, it will advance very far" (*W* 158). In order to belong wholly to Him, man must develop great generosity and detachment. The Saint—and this is the third piece of advice—insisted strongly on this. Otherwise, "if the Lord sees that after He places the kingdom of heaven in the soul's house this soul turns to earthly things, He will not only fail to show it the secrets there are in His kingdom but will seldom grant it this favor, and then for just a short space of time" (*W* 158–59).

Conclusion

This discussion has centered upon a prayer of quiet that flourishes during the time destined for prayer, but there is a

---

God, even though the work be of great service to God. For a little of this pure love is more precious to God and the soul and more beneficial to the Church, even though it seems one is doing nothing, than all these other works put together." In *Collected Works*, 523.

second form, one that continues in the midst of daily occupations. While one attends to the external service of God in discharging customary business, his will can remain united to Him. In this one feels that in his occupations, "the best part is lacking, that is, the will. The will, in my opinion, is then united with its God, and leaves the other faculties free to be occupied in what is for His service—and they then have much more ability for this. But in worldly matters, these faculties are dull and at times as though in a stupor" (*W* 155).

These experiences are very rewarding ones: "This is a great favor for those to whom the Lord grants it; the active and the contemplative lives are joined. . . . Thus Martha and Mary walk together" (*W* 155).

IV

The Gift of Self and
Unitive Contemplation

*"Thy will be done on earth
as it is in heaven"*

Chapter 32 is one of the most important chapters in the *Way of Perfection*. Commenting on the *Pater*, Saint Teresa had spoken of various degrees of prayer; here she began to discuss the perfect life in relation to the highest states of prayer. This chapter completes Teresa's commentary on the first part of the *Pater noster* and the exposition of the degrees of prayer.

The first paragraphs form a bridge with previous thought and set the tonality of the entire chapter, which is the Teresian atmosphere of generosity. Next follows a treatment of the importance of offering God one's will with its twofold effect: perfect or unitive contemplation and the state of union.

Since this chapter leads the reader to the summit of prayer, we might say that it is central in the *Way*.

We are aware of Saint Teresa's sense of the absolute. She did not like things done by halves; she wanted to give all and was convinced that God would help her in this and that He would even help her do greater things.

This is man's response to all that God has done for him.

God led Teresa to understand that He wished to give her His kingdom even in this life, wished to transform her into a heaven in which His perfect praise might continually resound. She recalled this gift which God offered her along with that of the divine sonship—affirmed in the first words of the *Pater noster*—and so she wanted to offer Him something in return. Jesus, Who taught us this great prayer and says it with us, offers to the Father, as a return gift, our will. A small thing, the will of His creature, but whoever gives it completely has given everything, because, in practice, the strength of the human personality rests in the will.

At this point, Teresa took to task those timid persons who dare not make this offering by saying *fiat voluntas tua*, because they fear being heard and receiving who knows what trials! If it is because of humility that they dare not say it, the Saint agreed, although she did observe that "He Who gives them love enough to ask for such a stern method of proving it will give them love enough to endure it" (chap. 32).

Importance of This Gift

"Before I tell you about what is gained, I want to explain the great deal you offer so that afterward you won't take back what you gave, claiming that you hadn't understood. . . . To say that we abandon our will to another's will seems very easy until through experience we realize that this is the hardest thing one can do" (*W* 161). It can happen at times that superiors ask things of us beyond our strength, because they do not realize our capacity. But God knows everything, and He will never demand anything we cannot do without the help of His grace, which will never be wanting.

This is one of the most beautiful pages in Saint Teresa's

writings. "I want to advise you and remind you what His will is. Don't fear that it means He will give you riches, or delights, or honors, or all these earthly things. His love for you is not that small" (*W* 162).

She left no doubt that there would be things to suffer; there is no human life without suffering: but it is part of God's plan. If He sends something to suffer, it is a sign of His predilection. Jesus passed this way; therefore, if a man is treated like Him, it is because he is loved by God: "He esteems highly what you give Him. He wants to repay you well, for He gives you His kingdom while you are still alive" (*W* 162).

There is a definite connection between the gift of the will and His kingdom. When one is generous, God is generous with him.

"Do you want to know how He answers those who say these words to Him sincerely? Ask His glorious Son, who said them while praying in the Garden. Since they were said with such determination and complete willingness, see if the Father's will wasn't done fully in Him through the trials, sorrows, injuries, and persecutions He suffered until His life came to an end through death on a cross" (*W* 162).

What will be His pleasure for those He loves? Certainly their sanctification, and so He will give them occasions to enrich themselves, showing them the footsteps of His Son and inviting them to follow the same road. "These are His gifts in this world." One does not become a saint without suffering, but when we do not think of the suffering, when (above all) we do not analyze it, we can suffer more generously. In suffering, one must look more at God than self and remember that He gives these gifts "according to the love He bears us: to those He loves more, He gives more of these gifts; to those He loves less, He gives less" (*W* 162).

Another rule is that suffering is always in proportion to love. "Whoever loves Him much will be able to suffer much for Him; whoever loves Him little will be capable of little. . . . The measure for being able to bear a large or small cross is love" (*W* 162).

The Saint concluded the first part of this chapter by saying: "Everything I have advised you about in this book is directed toward the complete gift of ourselves to the Creator, the surrender of our wills to His, and detachment from creatures" (*W* 163). Saint Teresa had a double aim in this book: to encourage man to consecrate himself entirely to God by the gift of his will and to detach it from creatures. The two things are complementary; the first cannot stand without the second. It is not possible to give oneself completely to God, always to do His will, without keeping all created things in their proper place.

But now for the consequences of this generous gift. Teresa did not enumerate them successively in distinct paragraphs, but they can be worked out by combining parts of the text. The soul

1. prepares itself in the best way for perfect contemplation;

2. is led to total transformation, that is to the *state* of transformation;

3. becomes powerful over the heart of God and obtains whatever it asks for the good of the Church and of souls because God gives back, so to speak, its will and takes pleasure in doing its wishes.

The Highest Degree of Prayer

The total gift of the will is the necessary condition for reaching perfect contemplation: by this offering, "We are prepar-

ing ourselves that we may quickly reach the end of our journey and drink the living water from the fount we mentioned", but "unless we give our wills entirely to the Lord
so that in everything pertaining to us He might do what conforms with His will, we will never be allowed to drink from
this fount" (*W* 163). Note here how perfect contemplation
is normally given to the soul that has made this surrender,
for we know that for Saint Teresa the foundation of living
water was the prayer of union, or perfect contemplation, as
she said explicitly: "Drinking from it is perfect contemplation, that which you told me to write about" (*W* 163).

The prayer of quiet is an approach to the fountain, a help
to reach unitive contemplation. If we correspond with this
first gift by the total gift of our will, so that "Your will,
Lord, be done in me in every way and manner that You,
my Lord, want" (*W* 163), then He will give the living water. He takes total possession of man who has put himself
completely into His hands and often gives him this prayer
of union—not always in the same measure, as we have observed in Saint Thérèse—but He certainly gives it, while
He gives it only by exception to those who have not yet
made this complete gift.

At this point, the Saint described a few characteristics of
perfect contemplation. First, it is completely passive: the
soul no longer contributes its own activity: "In this contemplation . . . we don't do anything ourselves. Neither do
we labor, nor do we bargain, nor is anything else necessary
—because everything else is an impediment and hindrance
—than to say *fiat voluntas tua*" (*W* 163).

Then: "The more our deeds show that these are not
merely polite words, all the more does the Lord bring us to
Himself and raise the soul from itself and all earthly things
so as to make it capable of receiving great favors" (*W* 164).
In the prayer of union, God can draw the soul so strongly

that it almost loses contact with surrounding life. "He never finishes repaying this service in the present life. He esteems it so highly that we do not ourselves know how to ask for ourselves, and His Majesty never tires of giving. Not content with having made this soul one with Himself, He begins to find His delight in it, reveal His secrets, and rejoice that it knows what it has gained and something of what He will give it. He makes it lose these exterior senses so that nothing will occupy it. This is rapture" (*W* 164).

These are contemplative graces. Teresa spoke of them only briefly; later she would explain them extensively in the *Interior Castle* in the Fifth and Sixth Dwelling Places. She wrote the *Castle* for spiritual directors and for those who experience such effects, so that they might be reassured when they see that they are not something strange. But here it did not seem necessary to her to speak of them in particular; it was enough to know that the other graces that can accompany perfect contemplation are only an intensification of the grace of the prayer of quiet, which was communicated by means of love, and that love is kindled more easily in one who is completely detached.

There is a close connection between progress in the life of perfection and development in the life of prayer. The divine light is diffused more abundantly in the center of the soul; as one grows more interior, he finds himself immersed in greater light and even becomes conscious of it and experiences it.

Therefore, the development of the spiritual life is, in a sense, closely related to the diverse kinds of prayer. It is true that the superior mystical prayers—of the Fifth, Sixth, and Seventh Dwelling Places—are not an integral part of the development of the spiritual organism, because they are not explained by the activity of the Holy Spirit alone; still, completely developed grace "disposes" the soul for these fruitive unions.

In the Fifth Dwelling Places, the union of the soul with God becomes total: from it flows a generous life in which one dies to himself to be reborn to divine life. In the two following dwelling places, this grace of union develops to the point of invading him totally and becoming habitual.

While she described the riches of the last dwelling places of the *Castle*, Saint Teresa affirmed that such graces were not of themselves necessary for sanctity and that God could bring souls to the perfect life without mystical union. The Holy Spirit's enlightenment, inseparable from sanctity, can be barely perceived at the same time that it deeply penetrates the life of the soul that has reached that state of perfection.

After all, the goal of the most elevated mystical graces is perfect love between the soul and God, and whoever truly loves is more drawn to give than to receive. Hence, precious as mystical union is, Saint Teresa always preferred union of conformity, moral perfection; she wished souls to dispose themselves for divine union by the perfect gift of themselves, by perfect conformity of their will with the will of God.

So we return again to the *gift of the will*.

Your will, Lord, be done in me in every way and manner that You, my Lord, want. If You want it to be done with trials, strengthen me and let them come; if with persecutions, illnesses, dishonors, and a lack of life's necessities, here I am; I will not turn away, my Father, nor is it right that I turn my back on You. Since Your Son gave You this will of mine in the name of all, there's no reason for any lack on my part. But grant me the favor of Your kingdom that I may do Your will, since He asked for this kingdom for me, and use me as You would Your own possession, in conformity with Your will. (*W* 164)

Saint Teresa, knowing her weakness and yet the greatness of the gift she should make, asked God to help her: Give me Thy kingdom, that is, the first form of contemplative prayer —the prayer of quiet of which she has already spoken—in such a way that I surrender myself in simply everything, fully trusting in You, and You may be able to dispose of me as You wish, for I am Yours, I do not belong to myself any longer.

After thus recalling what this gift consists of, she showed its second consequence, the transformation of the soul into God by love.

"What strength lies in this gift! It does nothing less, when accompanied by the necessary determination, than draw the Almighty so that He becomes one with our lowliness, transforms us into Himself, and effects a union of the Creator with the creature. Behold whether or not you are well paid" (*W* 164).

She clearly stated thus that the consequence of the total gift of our will to God is transformation. This really means the state of transformation that Saint John of the Cross places at the summit of perfection, the state in which the soul is divinized and acts in a divine manner because the will of God has taken complete possession of the soul and moves it in all and through all. In the Seventh Dwelling Places, Saint Teresa described the spiritual atmosphere in which this transformation of the soul is completed.

We know from Saint John of the Cross that there is question of a transformation of the will, which is transformed into the will of God, since it loves only what God loves. Hence it is an "affective" transformation of the soul. But if until now man was moved simply by the help of grace in the direction of the will of God, when he becomes perfect in love he is moved in this sense by the Holy Spirit. His transformation, therefore, besides being affective, in a certain sense is also effective, because his acts are divinized by the divine motion. This effective transformation proceeds from an intimate union that he feels in the depth of his being.

But the end of everything is always love, and Saint Teresa said that God's purpose in giving these graces is to strengthen us to imitate Christ in suffering. The soul pressed by love, though appreciating immensely God's gifts, does not stop at them, but is always anxious to give: he feels an immense need of repaying the divine generosity.

"To love, to be loved, to make love loved", this is the longing of the soul perfect in charity. Saint Thérèse reached this union, and this is the state in which God wishes to place our souls, also, but we must keep the door open by holding completely to the will of God.

Saint Teresa said that God is pleased to do the will of the soul: "He begins to commune with the soul in so intimate a friendship that He not only gives it back its own will but gives it His. For in so great a friendship the Lord takes joy in putting the soul in command, as they say, and He does what it asks since it does His will. And He does this even better than the soul itself could, for He is powerful and does whatever He wants and never stops wanting this" (*W* 164).

We find similar beautiful sentiments in Saint John of the Cross at the beginning of the third book of the *Ascent of Mount Carmel*:

> All the operations of the memory and other faculties in this state are divine. God now possesses the faculties as their complete lord, because of their transformation in Him. And consequently it is He Who divinely moves and commands them according to His spirit and will. As a result the operations are not different from those of God; but those the

soul performs are of God and are divine operations. Since he who is united with God is one spirit with Him . . . , the operations of the soul united with God are of the divine Spirit and are divine. . . .

God alone moves these souls to do those works that are in harmony with His will and ordinance, and they cannot be moved toward others. Thus the works and prayer of these souls always produce their effect. (Chap. 2, nos. 8 and 10, pp. 216–17)

V

God's Gift: The Eucharist

"Our daily bread"

An attentive reader of the *Way of Perfection* quickly notices that Saint Teresa devoted three entire chapters to the petition *Give us this day our daily bread*. And still more striking is her interpretation of this petition. For her, our daily bread is the Eucharist, and that explains her insistence: since she wanted to trace the way to perfection, she had to show the importance of the Blessed Sacrament in the pursuit of perfection. Saint Teresa, a realist, understood the value of the Eucharist: first of all, the real presence of Jesus and, then, Holy Communion.

The first of these three chapters treats of the gift of Jesus' presence among us, and the two following chapters, of sacramental Communion and spiritual communion.

Eucharistic Presence

In the first chapter (33), we note Teresa's effort to unite its thought with the preceding part on the total gift of the will to God; then she went on to the love of the heavenly Father and of Jesus Himself in giving the Eucharist and, finally, to the place It occupies in the Teresian concept of life.

Each of the first two paragraphs expressed the same thought: Jesus, in exhorting us to say *fiat voluntas tua*, has made us give a great deal, for He has us offer all our will to God's good pleasure, which is the same as a total gift of oneself and implies a reform of life.

Practical examples are given: "If we tell a rich person living in luxury that it is God's will that he be careful and use moderation at table so that others might at least have bread to eat, for they are dying of hunger, he will bring up a thousand reasons for not understanding this save in accordance with his own selfish purposes. If we tell a backbiter that it is God's will that he love his neighbor as himself, he will become impatient and no reason will suffice to make him understand" (*W* 165).

"What would happen if the Lord had not provided for us with the remedy He gave?" (*W* 166). Because He knows that this gift of our will is hard—and yet so important because it is the means to perfect charity—he desires to motivate us in making it by giving us a perpetual sign of His love.

The great manifestation of His love is in the Incarnation and in the Eucharist that perpetuates the Incarnation. The soul who lives by faith knows that Christ remains there to help us, that He invites us to Himself to give us strength, seeming to repeat to us: "Come to me, all who . . . are heavy laden, and I will give you rest" (Mt 11:28).

In the second paragraph, the Saint explained her thought more clearly: "Jesus observed what He had given for us, how important it was that we in turn give this, and the great difficulty there is in our doing so . . . since we are the way we are: inclined to base things and with so little love and courage that it was necessary for us to see His love and courage in order to be awakened—and not just once but every day. After He saw all this, He must have resolved to remain with us here below" (*W* 166).

The Eucharist is a manifestation, not only of Jesus' love, but also of the heavenly Father's. The Saint noted that Jesus asks the Father to be allowed to remain with us because He wishes to do only the Father's will and be humbly subject to Him: "He wanted, as it were, to ask permission [of His Father]" (*W* 166) for the gift of His permanent presence in the Eucharist. And in granting the permission, the Father does indeed show His love for us, for He knows we shall renew upon the Eucharist the thankless treatment we gave His Son when He was on earth.

Saint Teresa's catholic instinct appears in her appreciation of the Blessed Sacrament. She could not agree with the theologians who maintained that at a certain point in the mystical life one should leave Jesus. She could not conceive life without Jesus present in the Blessed Sacrament.

Sacramental Communion

Chapter 34 speaks about the meaning that Teresa gave the words *our bread*, that is, the Eucharistic bread, meaning not only Holy Communion but also the real presence of Jesus in the Blessed Sacrament, for He nourishes us by both. She wishes us to ask that Jesus remain with us always.

Speaking here to Carmelite nuns, whom in their Constitutions she told to trust that God would always provide for their necessities if they were good frugal religious, she exhorted them to disregard the other sense of these words that exegetes must consider, namely, material bread.

After that, she turned to the way we should receive Jesus in the Blessed Sacrament. It is interesting to note that the method suggested is supported by theology and is characteristic of a contemplative—preparing the way for Jesus to reveal Himself to the soul so that it might taste Him. It is a method based on theology, for it is an exercise of the theological virtues that put us in direct contact with God: faith and love. Both of these are activated by the will and in that sense are within our power.

Faith

To receive the grace that God wishes to bestow, one has to be receptive, and faith is the best means to it. Saint Teresa spoke of herself when she mentioned a person who had such a living faith that she "saw"—she meant with the eyes of faith—Our Lord coming to her in Communion and smiled at the thought of those who wanted to have lived in Palestine in His day to see Him. If she possessed Jesus in the Blessed Sacrament, there was nothing more to desire, her faith told her.

The exercise of faith depends on our will in a double manner: because we can make acts of faith when we wish and because the adhesion of the mind to the truth depends on our will. We believe because we wish to believe, and we can bring to this act a will inflamed with love; then faith becomes "a certainty dark but sure".

Saint Teresa invited her readers to concentrate all their attention at Communion time on the act of faith: to see Christ truly entering into them to keep them company, to be their food. This is not an imaginary picture such as one can make during his meditation, nor is it simply His operative presence by which He keeps man always under His influence; in Communion, Jesus is really present with His most holy Humanity. Therefore, the Saint noted, this is not the time to pray before a picture of Him, but to "see" Jesus really in us and to entertain ourselves with Him. Saint Teresa wished us to cultivate this gaze of faith diligently so that it might become ever more loving.

Love

Beside faith there must be love. Love of desire, of repentance, of union. The essential thing is that it open the soul wide to the great Eucharistic gift. God comes as doctor, and one can expose to Him all his spiritual necessities.

At Communion time, we are offered actual grace to love more. Jesus comes to unite Himself to us; so the right thing to do is to desire union, to ask Him for it. It is the motion of the Holy Spirit that makes this possible, and the theological virtues put us in the best dispositions to follow His movement.

It is no wonder that God makes Himself felt in a soul full of faith and love and gives it a great desire to be generous in His service. The feeling is not essential, but we shall be happy if at that time God gives us a grace of union, though keeping ourselves in great resignation. If we are faithful to recollection, Teresa wrote, "Though He comes disguised, the disguise . . . does not prevent Him from being recognized in many ways" (*W* 173).

Spiritual Communion

We call it "spiritual communion" to distinguish it from sacramental Communion, for the sacrament is not actually received in it. It is a great act of desire by which one invites Jesus into his heart and goes to meet Him.

Christ in the Eucharist brings not only the physical presence of His Humanity—which is certainly a special blessing, though from a spiritual point of view not the most important—but also an increase of grace, according to one's love.

Christ can give this fruit by His physical presence—in sacramental Communion—but this He also does when one has a great desire for Him to come into the soul to nourish it, or, in other words, a great desire to make the so-called spiritual communion.

Spiritual communion can be made by an act of simple desire in a moment, by a simple cry of the soul; or more at length, with an express formula of preparation and thanksgiving.

Saint Teresa recommended this practice heartily, but it must be employed with good judgment. It is excellent if one feels inspired to multiply these acts, but the soul must not tie itself down; there are other ways of begging God to visit and work in us.

We should note in this regard that Saint Teresa was thinking mainly of assistance at Mass. When one cannot receive sacramental Communion, let him nevertheless dispose himself as if he could, and when the priest communicates make a spiritual communion, with a fervent act of desire for Jesus to come and nourish love in him. But though Teresa spoke explicitly of participation at Holy Mass, we understand from the motives she gave that her recommendation holds also for occasions outside of Mass. Nor should one feel alarm because he experiences some difficulty with the practice: "Consider that if in the beginning you do not fare well (for it could be that the devil will make you feel afflicted and constrained in heart since he knows the great damage that will be caused him by this recollection), the devil will make you think you find more devotion in other things and less in this recollection after Communion. Do not abandon this practice; the Lord will see in it how much you love Him" (*W* 175).

Many do not consider spiritual communion important because they have never practiced it well. It is important to remember that any desire of union puts new vigor into the soul, and, therefore, it is well to profit by it.

In the second part of the chapter, we find an ardent exclamation of the Saint that reveals her desire to see Jesus honored in His sacrament. In her day, heretics attacked and profaned the Eucharist, and her spirit of reparation made her feel great joy each time she founded a new monastery and opened a new tabernacle. The presence of Jesus is always an occasion of grace for souls.

VI

Forgiving

"Forgive us our trespasses
as we forgive . . ."

Chapter 36 treats of man's reflecting God's mercy, that is, his love of others in imitation of the way God has always loved him despite all his weaknesses.

Pardon

After a brief explanation of the petition, Saint Teresa named what it is that we have to forgive. Sometimes God has permitted the saints to suffer great injuries or calumnies, and He could do the same to us to make us practice humility; but these are rare, and, therefore, it is not so much upon these that Teresa wished to fix our attention, but on others that happen much more frequently. She noted that there are little things in life that cause more suffering than great ones, because they touch us from closer at hand and more frequently; for the most part, these are slight injustices or hurts received in living together, differences of character, lack of attention, of delicacy, of education, and so on. These offenses may come from without, that is, from our surroundings, but they also come from within—from our self-love, "points of honor".

Saint Teresa spoke of the pardon of offenses as a great act of love, which God considers important, making His pardon depend on it: "How the Lord must esteem this love we have for one another! Indeed, Jesus could have put other virtues first and said: forgive us, Lord, because we do a great deal of penance or because we pray much and fast or because we have left all for You and love You very much. He didn't say forgive us because we would give up our lives for You, or, as I say, because of other possible things. But He said only, 'forgive us because we forgive' " (*W* 180).

The quality of forgiveness is a guarantee that one living a life of prayer is on the right road; it is a test of the authenticity of contemplative graces. Saint Teresa said she had found that contemplatives were always ready to pardon and love those who caused them difficulties. And she gave the reason: one growing in union with God becomes more and more aware of both His mercy and his own unworthiness, with the result that he acquires a merciful attitude toward others.

We find this quality in all the saints, and, in our day, Saint Thérèse has been a special messenger of merciful Love. She saw how God takes the initiative in His goodness; that gave her strength to overcome all the difficulties she encountered in the monastery.

A General Glance

Chapter 37 glances for a moment at the ground already covered and at that still remaining.

Saint Teresa recalled that the first petitions of the *Pater noster* afforded her an opportunity to discuss all the degrees of prayer from meditation to the prayer of union, the fount of living water. "Up to now the Lord has taught us the whole way of prayer and of high contemplation, from the beginning stages to mental prayer, to the prayer of quiet, and to that of union" (*W* 183).

Now she was to use the remaining petitions to explain the effects of prayer. "From here on, the Lord begins to teach us about the effects of His favors, as you have seen" (*W* 185). When prayer is authentic, it cannot fail to produce such effects.

Between prayer and virtue there is the relation of cause and effect. The effect of prayer is love; if this is produced, the prayer is good, otherwise it is weak. The love itself is twofold: love of God and love of neighbor. Love of God consists in saying always more deeply *fiat voluntas tua* and meaning it both actively and passively: passively, accepting all God does in us and about us as invitations He sends us to go to Him; and actively, generously doing all He asks of us.

For Saint Teresa, the practical test for seeing whether a soul truly loves God is charity toward his neighbor, a love based on his relations with God, not his personal qualities. Christ considers done to Himself all we do for our neighbor; it is in fraternal charity that the love of God becomes tangible.

The distinctive characteristic of the Christian is fraternal charity. The only instrument of the apostolate with which one goes to the very depth of the soul of those to be converted—and which, therefore, is efficacious—is that attitude of deep love which never fails, notwithstanding ingratitude.

If we treat our neighbor with the same delicacy we would use toward Christ, we possess the best proof that our love for

God is genuine. Even Saint Thomas says that if we cannot have metaphysical certainty of being in God's grace, we can have moral certainty, and this comes from testing our love for our neighbor. This is one of the most beautiful things Saint Teresa said.

There are degrees of love of neighbor, said the Saint, but in all of them there is present the pardoning of wrongs. "The perfect will give their will in the way perfect souls do and forgive with that perfection that was mentioned. We, Sisters, will do what we can; the Lord receives everything" (*W* 183–84). If one cultivates a complete surrender of himself to God's will that will show itself through fraternal charity, Saint Teresa assured us that God will recompense him in his prayer and bring him into His intimacy.

In this way, the Saint hinted at the theme of the next chapters: our life is a continual search for divine intimacy. But, while we are on this earth, we are surrounded by difficulties and temptations of the devil. Fragile as we are, we truly need protection from evil.

VII

Temptations

"And lead us not into temptation"

Under this heading Teresa wrote, not only of temptation, but of trials in general. But the examples she gave are of temptations, inasmuch as the trials are presented as occasions of not going toward God as directly as one ought. She said there is no need to be afraid of them: little by little as souls become more perfect, they have less fear of temptation and trials, because they know that love develops in suffering.

Saint Thérèse, during the period in which her sister Céline carried the heavy cross of caring for their gravely ill father, encouraged her by reminding her that trials are actually a sign of God's love for us. Therefore, perfect souls should desire them rather than ask to be freed from them, but they must also ask that temptation may not harm them.

This petition of the *Pater noster* might also be worded: "O God, do not let me surrender to temptation"; one does not ask not to have any temptations, but only not to be deceived by them. In fact, the enemy, profiting from the complexity of human nature, manages to keep temptation hidden until it has done harm. When a man has really given himself to our Lord, he cannot be deceived, but as long as he has inordinate self-love, fallen nature has a tendency to be blind to temptation.

False Spiritual Consolation

After outlining the meaning of this petition, Saint Teresa explained some temptations into which the soul can fall if it is not alert. She was speaking here mainly of those who live the life of prayer.

The devil can deceive us into believing that the consolations we have in prayer come from God when it is he who is producing them. Saint Teresa makes little of this temptation: when a person is humble and sincere, it cannot hurt him, for if he believes the consolations are from God, he will feel impelled to thank Him, and the enemy, seeing that he is losing his time, will end by leaving him in peace. The Saint recommended humility, however. One should not think he has any right to special consolations in prayer; they cannot be procured by his own efforts, and if he seeks them, he is preparing himself to be deceived.

I have always been struck by what Teresa said at the end of chapter 2 of the Fourth Dwelling Places of the *Interior Castle*. After teaching how one prepares for the prayer of quiet, she recommended: "After you have done what should be done by those in the previous dwelling places: humility! humility! By this means the Lord allows Himself to be conquered with regard to anything we want from Him. The first sign for seeing whether or not you have humility is that you do not think you deserve these favors and spiritual delights from the Lord or that you will receive them in your lifetime."[1] Not that the Saint was contradicting what she had already

[1] In vol. 2 of *The Collected Works of St. Teresa of Avila*, trans. Kieran Ka-

said: we remember that preceding chapters of the *Way of Perfection* have urged us—as far as lies in us, but without presumption—to prepare for contemplation and await it from God, Who will give it when and as He wills. The important thing is to know that there is no need to desire spiritual consolations; one who does not seek them is in the best disposition to receive the mercy of God, and, if he is always content with what God gives him, he cannot be deceived.

Another temptation, more serious and common, in persons who aspire to perfection and to acquiring virtues is to believe they possess them. This temptation is much more subtle and more dangerous than the other, because there a person believes he is receiving while here he thinks he is giving to God. He believes that he has rights over Him; he does not exert himself to acquire virtue, for he thinks he has it already, and so he grows weak.

Teresa drew from her own experience the counsels she gave for this case. She had many difficulties in practicing virtue, both from her physical condition and from the external circumstances of her life.

In the midst of all these difficulties, generous as she was, Teresa practiced virtue; and yet it is beautiful to see with what humility she confessed her weakness.

> At other times I think I have great courage and that I wouldn't turn from anything of service to God; and when put to the test, I do have this courage for some things. Another day will come in which I won't find the courage in me to kill even an ant for God if in doing so I'd meet with any opposition. In like manner it seems to me that I don't care at all about things or gossip said of me; and when I'm put to the

test this is at times true—indeed I am pleased about what
they say. Then there come days in which one word alone
distresses me, and I would want to leave the world because
it seems everything is a bother to me. . . . Who will be able
to say of himself that he is virtuous or rich? . . . No, Sisters, but let us always think we are poor. (*W* 187)

It would be a mistake to lean on our own presumed virtues
as if they were a solid foundation. Saint Teresa Margaret, for
example, struggled to the end of her life to acquire virtue,
even when she had already entered the mystical life.

Saint Teresa said that to remedy this temptation, one
should pray and nourish low sentiments of oneself, recalling that the virtues are gifts of God. Saint Thérèse gives a
good commentary on the holy Mother's thought when she
says that the virtues are treasures that the heavenly Father
has put into the hands of His child to use, but they always
remain His.

In fact, when the virtues grow in the soul, they always
grow because of a deepening of sanctifying grace, for the
virtues are "habits" of the soul. If we consider single acts
of virtue, we know that for each of them an actual grace is
necessary; to perform an act of heroic virtue, the gifts of
the Holy Spirit are needed: therefore, of ourselves we are
incapable of anything. The desires we feel at times in prayer
are good but are only the beginning of virtue; for virtue to
be effective, it must be put into action.

The Saint gave examples: the devil can make us believe we
possess patience, but put to the test, all this patience goes up
in smoke. Or we can form the habit of saying and believing
that we want nothing and do not care about anything, when
it is not really so. Therefore, Teresa recommended vigilance
and assured us that when a soul really acquires one virtue

perfectly, all the others come with it. That is the reason why spiritual writers advise concentrating all one's efforts on one virtue: laboring to acquire one, we labor to acquire them all.

False Humility

In chapter 39, Saint Teresa continued to discuss hidden temptations, like a false humility that throws the soul into disquiet. Humility is the virtue that puts things in their place, in order. Our place before God is that of children. When Christ wanted to teach humility, He called a child and showed it to the apostles, saying, "Unless you turn and become like children you will never enter the kingdom of heaven" (Mt 18:3). He wants us to be conscious of our littleness and weakness, but in the manner of the child who is afraid of a dog and throws itself into its mother's arms. From that safe refuge, it looks fearlessly at the beast, and we can do the same in regard to God and say: "Dear Lord, how I need You! I am hoping for everything from You!"

Sometimes distrustful sentiments flow simply from our own oversensitiveness and can be overcome, but the devil also may have a hand in them. Depression is an open door for him. He knows that disturbance lowers our power to love, and his aim is precisely to keep souls from progressing in the ways of love. He uses this snare especially on souls he cannot make fall into sin.

Therefore, the Saint put us on our guard: "Now be also on your guard, daughters, against some types of humility given by the devil in which great disquiet is felt about the gravity of our sins. This disturbance can afflict in many ways even to the point of making one give up receiving Communion and practicing private prayer. These things are given up because the devil makes one feel unworthy" (*W* 189).

Sister Marie of the Eucharist (Marie Guérin) became a joyous and serene person but first passed through these temptations even to the point of leaving Holy Communion. Her cousin, Saint Thérèse, urged her in a letter to trust and never to omit Communion for these fears.

Saint Teresa continued:

> When such persons approach the Blessed Sacrament, the time they used to spend in receiving favors is now spent in wondering whether or not they are well prepared. The situation gets so bad that the soul thinks God has abandoned it because of what it is; it almost doubts His mercy. Everything it deals with seems dangerous, and what it uses, however good, seems fruitless. It feels such distrust of itself that it folds its arms and remains idle; what is good in others seems evil when the soul sees it within its own self.
>
> Consider carefully, daughters, the matter I'm going to speak to you about, for sometimes it will be through humility and virtue that you hold yourselves to be so wretched, and at other times it will be a gross temptation. I know of this because I have gone through it. Humility does not disturb or disquiet or agitate, however great it may be; it comes with peace, delight, and calm. Even though a person upon seeing himself so wretched understands clearly that he merits to be in hell, suffers affliction, thinks everyone should in justice abhor him, and almost doesn't dare ask for mercy, his pain, if the humility is genuine, comes with a sweetness in itself and a satisfaction that he wouldn't want to be without. The pain of genuine humility doesn't agitate or afflict the soul; rather this humility expands it and enables it to serve God more. The other type of pain disturbs

everything, agitates everything, afflicts the entire soul, and
is very painful. I think the devil's aim is to make us think
we are humble and, in turn, if possible, make us lose con-
fidence in God. (*W* 189–90)

What did the Saint tell us to do? "When you find yourselves in this condition, stop thinking about your misery,
insofar as possible, and turn your thoughts to the mercy of
God, to how He loves us and suffered for us" (*W* 190). If
you cannot do even this, the only thing left is to have patience and offer your suffering to God.

Excessive Penance

Another temptation regards penances—that is, those done
outside obedience, for there is little danger of deception if
they are controlled by obedience.

Corporal penances are good and must be good for us, otherwise Saint Teresa would not have woven so much mortification into the life of her daughters. But they are only
an accompaniment of internal giving. I knew a good Mis-
tress of Novices who, when she noticed a novice wander-
ing from obedience a little, immediately took all penances
away from her, to make her understand that the gift of one's
own will comes first. It would be wrong to render oneself
incapable of fulfilling one's duties in order to do penance.
Bodily penance should be limited according to our duties
and our physique.

Therefore, the Saint did not approve of penances without
obedience.

One who does a penance he has been forbidden is obviously deluded. His penance—according to a strong expres-

sion of Saint John of the Cross[2]—would be the penance "of beasts".

Exaggerated Confidence

This temptation is the opposite of the one by which the soul lets itself be too depressed by its littleness; here it is too sure of itself and believes it will never fall again.

Saint Teresa wanted us to be determined not to commit a single mortal sin or even a deliberate venial sin, however small; but, notwithstanding this, we ought never to believe ourselves impeccable or trust ourselves, but only God; otherwise, we shall pay dearly. Saint Thérèse had already reached sanctity when, in her beautiful exposition of fraternal charity[3] commenting on the passages of the Gospel on charity, she mentions the many imperfect tendencies she experienced—though she had reached the state of perfection. This demonstrates that our nature is always wounded and carries within it the consequences of the original fall.

Finally, Saint Teresa repeated: "Lead us not into temptation" and begged God to free us from hidden temptations. She then ended the chapter with a little observation full of good sense in regard to the temptations that one meets in the life of prayer: that the world marvels at seeing persons who live the interior life tempted and deluded, while it pays no attention to the temptations worldly people have.

[2] Saint John of the Cross, *The Dark Night*, bk. 1, chap. 6, no. 2, in *The Collected Works of St. John of the Cross*, trans. Kieran Kavanaugh, O.C.D., and Otilio Rodriguez, O.C.D. (Washington, D.C.: ICS Publications, Institute of Carmelite Studies, 1979), 307.

[3] Saint Thérèse, *Story of a Soul*, chaps. 9 and 10.

VIII

Love and Fear God

To the temptations with which the devil tries to delude and frighten souls, slowing them down on the way of perfection, Saint Teresa opposed two remedies: love and fear. "Love will quicken our steps; fear will make us watch our steps to avoid falling along the way" (*W* 192). The fear is not the servile fear of a slave who dreads displeasing his master lest he be punished, but filial—that of the child who does not want to give the least pain to the father he loves. Saint John of the Cross makes this beautifully clear.[1]

Love in Contemplatives

Note how Saint Teresa introduced the theme: since love is the great remedy against temptations, it is very important to have it and to know that we have it.

Here it is evident that the Saint, in contact with the theologians of her time and, having among her directors learned men like the famous Dominican Father Bañez, was influenced by them to some extent. It was just after the close of the Council of Trent and the institution of the Roman

[1] Saint John of the Cross, *The Spiritual Canticle*, stanza 26, no. 3.

Congregation of the Council to introduce its teaching and practice everywhere. The subject of grace had been treated in the Council, and the question of the certainty of possessing it had been discussed. We can see traces of this here.

The Saint spoke with theological exactitude, her keen mind understanding that, since to possess grace and to have charity is the same thing, if one were certain of possessing love, he would also be certain of having grace. However, theologians do teach—and the theologians of Salamanca are perhaps the ones who have thrown the greatest light on the point—that if we cannot have mathematical certitude, based on evidence, we can have moral, practical certainty. And the Saint did add: "But reflect, Sisters, that there are some signs that even the blind, it seems, see. They are manifest signs, though you may not want to recognize them. They cry out loudly" (*W* 192).

This is the teaching of Saint Thomas, commented on by the Salamanticenses, who teach that the soul can have practical proofs of possessing love and therefore of being in the state of grace, in such a way as to proceed with serenity.

Teresa gave some of these signs: "Those who truly love God, love every good, desire every good, favor every good, praise every good. They always join, favor, and defend good people. They have no love for anything but truth and whatever is worthy of love" (*W* 192). They are souls whom nothing interests anymore except the things of God; this is evident proof that they belong to God and have no attachment to the world.

It is a pleasure to notice that, speaking of this tendency toward all that is good, toward what concerns the glory of God, Saint Teresa names works of the most exquisite charity, that is, helping one's neighbor in things that refer to the service of God. In the *Interior Castle*, she indicates charity for our neighbor as proof that we possess the love of God.[2]

One who is occupied only with the things of God cannot be interested in those of the world any longer.

> Do you think it is possible for a person who really loves God to love vanities? No, indeed, he cannot; nor can he love riches, or worldly things, or delights, or honors, or strife, or envy. All of this is so because he seeks only to please the Beloved. These persons go about dying so that their Beloved might love them, and thus they dedicate their lives to learning how they might please Him more. Hide itself? Oh, with regard to the love of God—if it is genuine love—this is impossible. If you don't think so, look at St. Paul or the Magdalene. Within three days the one began to realize that he was sick with love; that was St. Paul. The Magdalene knew from the first day; and how well she knew! Love has this characteristic: it can be greater or lesser in degree. Thus the love makes itself known according to its intensity. When slight, it shows itself but slightly; when strong, it shows itself strongly. But where there is love of God, whether little or great, it is always recognized. (*W* 192–93)

This love, then, rouses in the soul the single preoccupation: God! When she finds this sign in herself, for all practical purposes she is certain she has the love of God.

The Saint was speaking to contemplatives and insisted that their love must not be weak; it must be strong; it is the substratum of contemplation, and a certain intensity of love is always supposed by the contemplative light that makes one penetrate into God by experience of love, not by ideas. Saint John of the Cross, speaking of the spiritual marriage,

---

[2] Saint Teresa of Jesus, *Interior Castle*, V, chap. 3, no. 8.

emphasized that this state supposes a strong love, acquired by the soul under the divine influence.[3]

This must be manifested by a great interior drive toward the things of God. This is a guarantee that the contemplative graces that the soul receives truly come from God.

This certainty is very important because the devil tries to raise vain fears; he is always a sower of disturbance, because that keeps a person from complete self-possession and concentration on God. Thus the devil, if he cannot make a person sin, tries at least to retard him, and that he does in two ways:

1. by inspiring fear of a life of prayer and
2. by lowering our idea of God's goodness.

The Nourishment of Love

If love is so important, how are we to make it grow? One great help is the conviction that our love is returned. When the soul seeks God, much more does He seek the soul;[4] if the soul loves God, much more does the Lord love it. The foundation of our love, said Saint Teresa, "is made from the cement of being repaid by another love[.] This other love can no longer be doubted since it was shown so openly and with so many sufferings and trials, and with the shedding of blood even to the point of death in order that we might have no doubt about it" (*W*194).

Revelation teaches us that the Incarnation, grace, the sacraments, and the Eucharist are obvious signs of the great love of God for us. And these mysteries that are taught by the catechism and continually recalled by the liturgy are a strong stimulus to love of God. Let us call attention to the union

[3] Saint John of the Cross, *Spiritual Canticle*, stanza 30, no. 11.
[4] Saint John of the Cross, *The Living Flame of Love*, stanza 3, no. 28.

between dogma and mysticism: on one side the certainty of faith, on the other the contemplative experience that drives one to penetrate into those mysteries.

Many are the advantages of perfect love, but the Saint indicated one especially: the tranquility of the soul in facing death. "May it please His Majesty to give us His love before He takes us out of this life, for it will be a great thing at the hour of death to see that we are going to be judged by the One whom we have loved above all things. We shall be able to proceed securely with the judgment concerning our debts. It will not be like going to a foreign country but like going to our own, because it is the country of one whom we love so much and who loves us" (*W* 194–95).

And then Teresa's apostolic spirit reminded her of those who do not live by this love and made her pity their sad lot —a new spur to live a life of perfect love.

Concluding the chapter, she mentioned the death of one who has reached the fullness of the spiritual life: "Let us not desire delights, daughters; we are well-off here; the bad inn lasts for only a night. Let us praise God; let us force ourselves to do penance in this life. How sweet will be the death of one who has done penance for all his sins, of one who won't have to go to purgatory!" (*W* 195). She meant the soul who has reached the transformation of love, who at times, under the impulse of the Holy Spirit, feels a longing for heaven and whose death is produced, not so much by a physical cause, as by one of those impulses of love which finally separates the soul from the body, as Saint John of the Cross said so well.[5] And Saint Teresa: "Even from here below you can begin to enjoy glory! You will find no fear within yourself but complete peace" (*W* 195).

[5] Ibid., stanza 1, no. 30.

Fear of God

The other weapon against temptations is the fear that is a gift of the Holy Spirit, like wisdom. When this fear is perfect, love is perfect, too. Teresa followed the same order in explaining it as she did for love: its manifestation, the means for acquiring it, and its benefits.

Fear does not mature suddenly; only gradually does it become robust and strong. "But once the soul has reached contemplation . . . the fear of God also, as with love, becomes very manifest; it doesn't disguise itself even exteriorly" (*W* 196).

Since the Saint was writing mainly for contemplatives, she described the characteristics that fear assumes in these souls, already become intimate friends of God. "Despite the fact that you may watch these persons very carefully, you will not see them become careless. For no matter how long we observe them, the Lord keeps them in such a way that even if a thing very much to their own interest comes along, they will not advertently commit a venial sin; mortal sins they fear like fire" (*W* 196–97), for in contemplation there is the special help of the Holy Spirit, Who guides and sustains the soul.

She said they would not *knowingly* commit one venial sin, that is, deliberately, consciously. And the same is true of deliberate imperfections, for in practice we should not make a distinction between venial sin and imperfection, though theologically there is a difference.

There are venial sins that escape our notice: "[Be] most careful not to commit venial sins—that is, advertently; for otherwise, who can go without committing many?" (*W* 197). There is question, naturally, of little things that do not displease God. "But there is an advertence that is very deliberate; another that comes so quickly that committing the venial sin and adverting to it happen almost together" (*W* 197). We have been taken by surprise; in our weakness and frailty, "we don't first realize what we are doing" (*W* 197).

This can happen even to saintly souls. Saint Teresa confessed a fault of this kind, committed one day during the last months of her life, when, feverish and wasted with disease as she was, she felt impatience at an indiscreet request of one of the sisters and showed it in the expression of her countenance. She accused herself of it to Mother Agnes in a little note, rejoicing—in her exquisite humility—at having been seen imperfect.

We ought never to be shocked at our frailty: the smaller we are, provided we admit it, the more will God come to meet us and do His work Himself. Venial sins of this kind are often occasions of great virtue for the soul.

Voluntary venial sins are quite another thing. To do with eyes open the least thing we know God does not want would be a horrible thing. "But from any very deliberate sin, however small it be, may God deliver us. . . . It doesn't seem to me possible that something like this can be called little, however light the fault; but it's serious, very serious" (*W* 197) from love's point of view.

Theologians say that voluntary venial sin cools charity in the soul. Charity's fervor is a firm will to please God; voluntary venial sins is the opposite: the will stops its flight toward God, or at least lowers it. So a fault can be very small but have serious consequences. Therefore, one must be firmly resolved to commit no voluntary fault.

How the Fear of God Is Gained

"Consider, Sisters, for the love of God, if you want to gain this fear of the Lord, that it is very helpful to understand the seriousness of an offense against God" (*W* 197–98).

Saint Ignatius had good reason to place the meditation on sin in the first part of his Exercises; it is precisely by considering what displeases God that we shall acquire this fear and that love of God will develop in us. "It's very necessary that this fear be deeply impressed within the soul. Such fear is easy to obtain if there is true love" (*W* 198). The fear of God is the flowering of that love which wishes to cling completely to the will of God. A soul who loves God fears to go contrary to the divine will even in the least thing; therefore, this holy fear is a sign of the love of God.

The filial fear of God bears great fruit in man. First, it puts hell under his feet, because the devils can no longer harm him. Their aim is to draw him away from God by sin, and this they cannot do if he is determined not to offend Him, cost what it may.

A holy liberty of spirit is born in such a soul.

Before he reached this determination, he had to be continually on the watch because any encounter might have been an occasion of sin for him. His fear was spiritual, yes, but not perfectly and solely filial: he was still a little afraid of displeasing others, and this made him somewhat clumsy and constrained; now he can be less timid. He has no human respect because he does not fear showing that he is all God's and acts with full freedom. Saint Teresa left us a beautiful example of this freedom from constraint in her own life, for everyone knows how simple, affable, and natural she was with those with whom she dealt.

When we understand this that I said about ourselves, there will be no need to go about so tense and constrained; the Lord will protect us, and the habit acquired will now be a help against offending Him. The need instead will be to go about with a holy freedom, conversing with those who are good even though they may be somewhat worldly. For those who, before you possessed this authentic fear of God, were a poison and a means of killing the soul will afterward often be a help to your loving and praising God more because He has freed you from that which you recognize as a glaring danger. If previously you played a part in contributing to their weaknesses, now by your mere presence you contribute to their restraint; this happens without their having any idea of paying you honor. . . .

So, Sisters, strive as much as you can, without offense to God, to be affable and understanding in such a way that everyone you talk to will love your conversation and desire your manner of living and acting, and not be frightened and intimidated by virtue. (*W* 198–99)

IX

Desire for Heaven

"But deliver us from evil. Amen."

One may ask to be delivered from evil, for Christ Himself taught us to ask for it. Saint Teresa noted this and desired to be exempt, but we shall see what she meant by evil.

To understand her interpretation, we have to remember the point in the spiritual life that she had reached when she was writing the *Way*. If I may give my opinion, I believe that if she had written fourteen or fifteen years later, she would not have spoken of "evil" as referring to earthly life, for then, having reached the state of spiritual marriage that she describes so well in the Seventh Dwelling Places, her thought in regard to the present life would have undergone a change.

The *Way* was written in 1562, when she had not yet reached the spiritual marriage; she was in the state of spiritual betrothal,[1] a state that is still subject to miseries, on

---

[1] Saint Teresa compares the three stages of the soul's spiritual progress in the mystical union to the three periods of the nuptial union: the first meetings, the betrothal, and the marriage.

Saint John of the Cross uses the same allegorical language. In his teaching, "the unitive way has two stages. The first, the spiritual betrothal, is designated 'the perfect and total *yes* that the soul says to the will of God', the perfect 'consent' with which the will adheres not only to what God commands, but

account of which she desired to be freed from the evils of life and to go to heaven.

Teresa spoke of both physical and moral evils and said decidedly (Escorial MS) that we do not mean to ask God to free us from the former, that is, hardships, sickness, suffering, and so on, which can even be of great advantage to us. Persons of the world may do this, but for a soul of prayer, there is no question of asking exemption from these sufferings, for she knows how to make a treasure of them. It is from the moral miseries that such a soul asks to be freed; that is, our weakness before the divine invitations, an evil from which it is hard to be completely free while we are on this earth.

"What good do we find in this life, Sisters, since we lack

---

also to what He desires, cost what it may. God answers this *yes* by giving the soul perfect virtues; but these are still not enough to 'arm' the sensible part fully, and the soul, though wholly given to God with her will, cannot yet always manage to draw her sensibility with her. The 'transformation' of the soul therefore is limited to the will, of which God is now master, and He often comes to 'visit' His 'betrothed' with contemplation that has now become luminous.

"He alone can introduce her into the spiritual marriage. Here the transformation becomes 'total': not only the will, but all the faculties are impelled by the love of God, which has become the soul's only motive in all it does; the sensibility is now no longer rebellious, but joins the spirit in a harmonious concert of all the faculties glorifying God. To love is the only exercise of the soul, and to love that God Whom she feels within her is the principle that moves her.

"She says with St. Paul: 'I live now not I, but Christ lives in me', and Christ shows her in the contemplative light the grandeurs of the Incarnation and of the Redemption. The Spouse of the Incarnate Word should know Him intimately and, with Him, His works, to which she should be most closely associated. For the rest, nothing can associate her to the redemptive work more closely than love. Under the impulse of divine love, then, the soul succeeds in loving God with a 'divine' love, reaches equality of love, and shares spiritually in the life of the Trinity" (from our article "The Doctor", *Vita Carmelitana*, no. 4 [November 1942]).

so much good and are absent from Him? Deliver me, Lord, from this shadow of death, deliver me from so many trials, deliver me from so many sufferings, deliver me from so many changes. . . . Deliver me now from all evil and be pleased to bring me to the place where all blessings are" (*W* 201-2). In her delicate desire not to give God the least displeasure, she would have preferred to be no longer in the present life, where she could still offend God; she desired to go to heaven.

But this spontaneous desire disappeared when she was established in the state of transforming union. While writing the *Way*, Saint Teresa was like the soul described by Saint John of the Cross at the beginning of the *Canticle*,[2] who seeks union with God and, desiring nothing but to love Him, asks to be freed from what keeps her from loving Him fully. Therefore, the evil from which she asks to be freed is life itself, in which God can still be lost and which does not permit us to enjoy our Lord continually.

The Saint spoke expressly of those who have tasted God in contemplation, an enjoyment that spurs them to glorify God and desire death as the means to reach the fullness of life. "They do not want to remain in a life where there are these many obstacles to the enjoyment of so much good" (*W* 202); but seeing that they do not die, they die because they cannot die.

Saint Teresa reached the spiritual marriage in the year 1572 and lived in this state ten years. Fully matured, a man in this state receives the gift of the perfect dominion of God in his entire being that, though leaving in him the sense

[2] Saint John of the Cross, *The Spiritual Canticle*, Stanza 1: "Where have You hidden, Beloved?", in *The Collected Works of St. John of the Cross*, trans. Kieran Kavanaugh, O.C.D., and Otilio Rodriguez, O.C.D. (Washington, D.C.: ICS Publications, Institute of Carmelite Studies, 1979), 416.

of his own littleness, makes virtue strong. He feels himself carried along by God, his weakness united to the strength of God; and thence he experiences deep peace. He does not think of himself any more, but of what he can do in Him Who strengthens him, as Saint Paul says. He is confirmed in grace, assured that he will nevermore lose God's friendship. Knowing that by living on this earth in the midst of sufferings and sacrifices, he can acquire a higher degree of love, he desires to go on suffering, for the degree of love that he will have at the moment of death will remain for all eternity.

Saint Teresa certainly did not lack sufferings, physical or moral, in the last years of her life. She suffered even at the hands of her family: her cousin, Sister Mary Baptist, and her niece, Teresita, grew cold toward her. Despite all these sorrows, however, we see her soul in complete serenity, all surrendered to God. In her last *Relation* (1581, to Don Alonso Velazquez, Bishop of Osma), she portrayed her soul in her last years. It was established in deep peace. Her only desire, she said, was to do the will of God: "This surrender to the will of God is so powerful that the soul wants neither death nor life, unless for a short time when it longs to die to see God."[3] Only under the action of the Holy Spirit, when she was caught in the current of divine love, did she desire death to arrive at the fullness of life, at the complete possession of the Blessed Trinity—an experience described by Saint John of the Cross in the *Flame*: "Tear through the veil of this sweet encounter!"[4] But other than these impulses, Teresa

---

[3] Saint Teresa of Jesus, *Spiritual Testimonies*, no. 65, 9, in vol. 1 of *The Collected Works of St. Teresa of Avila*, trans. Kieran Kavanaugh, O.C.D., and Otilio Rodriguez, O.C.D. (Washington, D.C.: ICS Publications, Institute of Carmelite Studies, 1976), 365.

[4] Saint John of the Cross, *The Living Flame of Love*, stanza 1, in *Collected Works*, 578.

lived in the fullest surrender. Earthly life, then, is no longer an evil, but the occasion of growing in love.

Saint Teresa closed her exposition of the last petition of the *Pater* with the desire for heaven. The life of heaven is simply the honor and glory of God, and the thought of it made her exclaim here: "Oh, how different this life would have to be in order for one not to desire death!" (*W* 202). But for the soul who reaches transformation in God by love, even the present life becomes a heaven: it is eternal life begun.

Conclusion

On the last two pages of the *Way of Perfection*, Saint Teresa reviewed the whole book and then allowed her soul to express itself spontaneously.

What struck her in this retrospective glance was that God had made her understand what profound doctrine the *Pater noster* contained: the whole way of perfection, from the beginning to when the soul drinks of the fount of living water.

She understood the way of perfection as a contemplative way that led to the divine union toward which she oriented the souls God confided to her, though she knew that not all would receive the grace of contemplation in the same way. Therefore, when she mentioned perfect contemplation, she referred to the book of her *Life* to complete what she did not explain in much detail in the *Way*. In the latter, she spoke of the lower grades of prayer including the prayer of quiet, thus opening a passage to the higher grades. If she had written the *Way* later on, she would have referred to the *Interior Castle*, where she synthesized the doctrine of prayer that she had already given in previous writings.

She was convinced that it had been our Lord Who had taught her what depths there were in the *Pater noster*, and she praised Him for it: "Now see, Sisters, how the Lord by giving me understanding of the great deal we ask for when reciting this evangelical prayer has removed the difficulty involved in my teaching you and myself the path that I began to explain to you. May He be blessed forever! Certainly it never entered my mind that this prayer contained so many deep secrets; for now you have seen the entire spiritual way contained in it, from the beginning stages until God engulfs the soul and gives it to drink abundantly from the fount of living water, which He said was to be found at the end of the way" (*W* 203).

We, too, can now take a unified view of the beautiful structure of the *Way*. In the first three chapters, Saint Teresa sketched the ideal of union with God that is realized above all through continual prayer. But with all her experience and discernment, she knew that to speak of contemplation without laying the sure foundation of virtue was to build on sand; therefore, from chapter 4 to 15, she spoke very practically of the virtues she considered basic: charity, detachment from everything and from oneself, humility. On this solid foundation, she sketched the way, the degrees of prayer, affirming that if one prepared himself with diligence, God would permit him to drink of that fount of living water which is contemplation. Not all would drink in the same way and in the same measure, but to all God would certainly give to drink: He would not satiate all at the rivers, but at least He would give them some drops and never permit them to die of thirst.

It matters little whether God makes His action felt or not, but it is certain that if one disposes himself, He will come to help him. God has not promised to give the prayer of quiet to everyone, but He will give His inspirations, and it is quite probable that He will really give infused prayer if one continues to prepare himself by practicing not only virtue but also prayer, really meaning it when he says: *Fiat voluntas tua!*

The Saint was pleased with the book she had just finished. But she made little of her part in it and turned to glorifying

God: "His Majesty knows well that my intellect would not have been capable of it if He had not taught me what I have said" (*W* 204). And if it was only right for the nuns who first received this masterpiece to be grateful to God, we too may thank Him for such a practical guide to spiritual perfection.

"May the Lord be blessed and praised; from Him comes every good we speak of, think about, and do" (*W* 204). As we pursue the way of prayer, we shall learn by experience that anything good there is in us comes from God, and we shall refer everything to Him alone.